BOB PERRY

Lifting the Lid on a

# BABY BOOMER'S

memory box

## ONE BOY'S LIFE AND TIMES

novum pro

All rights of distribution, including via film, radio, and television, photomechanical reproduction, audio storage media, electronic data storage media, and the reprinting of portions of text, are reserved.

Printed in the European Union on environmentally friendly, chlorine- and acid-free paper.

© 2024 novum publishing

ISBN 978-3-99146-799-1
Editing: Chris Beale
Cover photo:
Maksym Chub | Dreamstime.com
Cover design, layout & typesetting:
novum publishing
Author's photo:
Bob Perry, private collection

**www.novum-publishing.co.uk**

# Content


> *The Clean Air Act, suburban estates, high rise housing solutions and prefabs.*


> *Nuclear stockpiles. Home births and local politics. The Suez crisis, Nasser, and the Aswan dam. The Soviet invasion of Hungary.*


> *The funeral of King George VI. Legacies of war: Anderson shelters and rationing. The National Health Service in operation.*


> *Trade union power and industrial disputes. Beer and Sandwiches. Local politics.*

# Acknowledgement

To Steph, Jon, Alex, Caleb and Luca. You mean everything to me. Thanks Tim. I am grateful to enjoy your friendship and I am so glad that you were there to share my boyhood journey. I am also fortunate to have so many good friends. God bless you all.

In loving memory of Don Perry (1925–2007) and Doreen Perry (1931–2020).

# An introduction

I love my children and grandchildren and together we share the same world. There is however a big difference between us. While they are natives of this world, I feel like a temporary resident. I am a little out of place, or more accurately, a little out of time. The transformational changes that are so evident in everyday life, like sophisticated technological advances and changing social norms, take some adjusting to. I find myself alternating between being delighted, baffled, or, on occasion, frustrated. Familiar things from my childhood remain but now seem different. For example, factories still operate, and shops are stocked ready for sale. The big change is that things seem to happen with so little human involvement. Goods continue to be produced, and business is still transacted, but now these processes are unfettered by the world's different time zones and outdated concepts such as 'normal working hours'. Despite these apparent 24/7 operations, it is sometimes difficult to speak directly to 'real' people. When making purchases over the internet, I have myself been asked to confirm that I am not a robot!

Of course, life has been made simpler in many ways by technology, and for those willing to participate, it offers platforms for shopping, banking, and communication. Live news feeds offer immediacy, making the way in which I once received news seem pedestrian. The downside is that live news produces simultaneous comments, some of which may be ill-judged, leading to cyber bullying and unfounded conspiracy theories. The technology itself disregards national borders while drawing together a digital community into a global village of trading and communication. This produces the mixed blessing of denting parochial and nationalistic perspectives of the past, but at the expense of eroding long-held values and local cultures. An exponential change in part driven by technology has taken place within this country in terms of values, attitudes, and expectations from when I was young.

I have inhabited a vastly different world from the present one. I was born into a simpler place and time, an era that pre-dated moon landings, personal computers, mobile phones, and the use of the internet. When I was born not every household owned a car, a telephone landline, or even a refrigerator. I lived in a world that went by in a less complicated, seemingly more innocent way. This was a world where news, business and conversations were slower, more measured but by comparison limited. Friends were fewer, certainly, when compared with the count on Facebook, but they required the commitment of personal interaction. Adults networked by chatting to those around them in a queue, on a bus or waiting in a doctor's surgery. My early knowledge and views were shaped by listening to conversations in the street, over the dining table, at school, during Sunday school lessons and at the 'Common', a patch of greenery at the end of the road.

Growing up you get used to hearing the sage sayings of adults. One was 'there's no time like the present', which was meant to stress the opportunity for taking immediate action. In retrospect, the phrase could have been taken literally, the fifties and sixties were unlike any other period of history. It was a time that now seems quirky, lacking sophistication and dated, yet seismic changes were going on while I went about day-to-day life. Like fellow 'baby boomers[1]', I lived through a unique slice of time. The world I knew as a child was markedly different from anything that had gone before.

This was a period of huge change and achievement, with much to celebrate. As a society we had harnessed the potential of electricity, acquired clean water, benefitted from penicillin and other medicines, and established the National Health Service (NHS).

---

1 A baby boomer is someone born between the end of the Second World War and the mid nineteen sixties.

Rationing was finally being shaken off. The First World War, 1914–1918, was meant to be a war to end all wars. Such optimism was not well placed as another world war was being fought against the same enemy a little over twenty years later. Emerging from these conflicts on the winning side there was a new opportunity for lasting peace. To this end, a Western European alliance of nations, now known as the European Union (EU), offered potential for not only security but also trade[2]. Crime rates were down, housebuilding by both the public and private sectors was a reality, and successive governments were committed to a general policy of full employment. Despite high personal taxation, there was an undeniable truth in the words of a Prime Minister of the period that, as a nation, we had 'never had it so good'[3]. A step change in technological advancement was taking place and consumerism was starting to take hold. For the right price new types of appliances for the home could make cooking, cleaning, and washing less of a chore. The cinema and theatre as sources of entertainment could, for a fee, be supplemented by ownership of a radio or television set. For those whose pockets were not deep enough, there was credit in the form of the hire purchase (HP) agreements. The 'never, never' promised jam today and the maxim of 'never a lender or borrower be' belonged to an earlier generation. For the first time ever there was widespread ownership of a revolutionary form of personal transport, the motor car.

Life however was not lived under permanent blue skies, there was something of a permanent, sinister shadow, some might say a very dark cloud. A 'Cold War' between two rival political ideologies, capitalism and communism, was raging. Far from being just a noisy disagreement, there was a deep mutual distrust and a real fear of the threat of mass nuclear destruction. As well as stockpiling

---

2 Although Britain did not join the six founding countries until 1973 before voting to leave in 2016.

3 Harold Macmillan who was Prime Minister from 1957 to 1963.

weapons, the Cold War also spawned intriguing tales of spy networks and secret agents. A space race between the two sides got underway unofficially to confirm which 'ism' had superiority.

Aside from a fear that the nuclear button might be pressed there was much for the nation to wrestle with. Britain may have emerged from the Second World War victorious a decade earlier, but it was nearly bankrupt. The Americans were owed billions of pounds and were now calling in their debts. Any sort of economic progress was inevitably impeded by this burden, indeed, governments feared real hardship and secret plans to avoid starvation were considered necessary. The magnitude of our indebtedness meant that the country was by necessity politically tied to its transatlantic paymaster. Then there was the legacy of once being a colonial power. At its peak, one in four of the world's population belonged to the British Empire. (A huge map on the wall of my classroom evidenced as much with great swathes of countries coloured pink.) Running an empire came at a cost both financial and moral. Now immigration from the Commonwealth was becoming a source of social tension in some parts of the country.

These are some of the headlines from the world of 'then'. I lived through it all in a kindly subculture on a new suburban Black Country estate. Experiences of childhood, early relationships, family and how you are raised all help shape your moral code, what you believe and ultimately who you are. Societies are built on stories such as mine. Reflecting on these stories helps me make sense of my place in a world I once lived in and how today's world has been shaped by the past. It was a Danish philosopher of a century earlier who observed that life can only be understood backwards but must be lived forwards[4].

Certain trivial items and customs have faded completely from use over the years. I can remember *Smiths* crisps being sold as

---

4  Soren Kierkegaard (1813–1855).

unsalted, but packets came with a small blue packet of salt inside. Then there were toys that were just plain dangerous, including lead soldiers, *Meccano* construction kits with sharp metal edges and toy cannons that fired match sticks with far too much power. Children's toothpaste was different. *Gibbs* toothpaste was sold in a round metal tin and had the texture of brittle boot polish, and significantly came in a choice of pink and lime green colours. The big autumn event for children was always November fifth, when the thwarting of the 1605 gunpowder plot to blow up parliament was celebrated. In addition to the sale of fireworks, bonfires were lit, and this tradition carries on normally in back gardens, rarely at organised events. We often went to a distant cousin's home whose daughter Wendy celebrated her birthday on that day. No bonfire was complete without a scarecrow-type effigy of Guy Fawkes (one of the gunpowder plotters) being placed on the top of the bonfire pile. In the run up to the big night, children would lay their guys on the floor in prominent places such as street corners and outside pubs and ask passers by, 'A penny for the guy?'. Coins and loose change could be exchanged for fireworks for the big night. This practice seems to have died out completely, being replaced by the American imports of trick-or-treat and Halloween celebrations. I could recount many more examples; I am just illustrating the fact that I lived in a world that is now fast disappearing.

This is my story of an unremarkable upbringing in Britain of the nineteen fifties and sixties. My reminiscences might be considered overly personal, nostalgic, or sentimental. They are, however genuine and echo everyone's story who lived through this period of history. For those much younger it is an opportunity to open the lid on a time capsule or open a door into another world. This is my attempt to sketch a ghost before it disappears from the room[5].

---

5 An expression I have borrowed from author Daniel Gray.

# THE BACK STORY

# Chapter One

## *No place like home*

There is a place where a meandering Cherry Tree Avenue joins Maple Drive and Greenside Way. Almond Avenue and Lilac Avenue dissect the lazy loop of the road like tributaries to a mighty river. Road names such as these may conjure an image of a rural idyll, a quiet, green hamlet festooned with multiple varieties of trees. The reality is different. These roads form part of Yew Tree Estate, a community of some twelve thousand souls. Despite the naming policy, when it was first built the Estate was devoid of trees apart from a few on the common ground at the end of the road. Instead of tree-lined pavements, residents looked out on tar-encrusted telegraph poles and lampposts of concrete. This is where I was born and grew up.

Long ago there was a sliver of time where everything changed forever, a period when the physical and social landscape of the nation was indelibly redrawn. Sometime in the eighteenth century, a heady combination of imagination, innovation and inventions combined to herald in an era now known as the Industrial Revolution. The capital of entrepreneurs and the creative insight of inventors may have driven industrialisation, but it was powered by the exploitation of the potential of steam power, fossil fuel reserves and the labour of ordinary working people. Rural, agricultural life and homemade wares gave way to the efficiencies of dark factories. The revolution brought with it immense wealth for factory owners, mass-produced textiles and metal products, and crowded towns. Even today, eight out of ten people in England live in an urban environment. The Yew Tree Estate I once knew was neither country nor was it urban. It was in fact a purpose-built suburbia where the Black Country conurbations of Walsall and Sandwell touch.

Nothing could point to, highlight, underline, and double-underline Britain's industrial heritage more than the Black Country[6]. The area was already long known for its metalworking industries and rich seams of coal and limestone. Advances in manufacturing technology, and the capability of new machinery offered the potential for exponential growth in these and other activities. The first commercially useful steam engine[7] was built in the area, but there was still a need for the country's most landlocked region to get products to market. The answer lay in the development of an efficient canal network that offered unhindered transport of goods and materials. The breakthrough happened in 1769 when canal engineering genius James Brindley's vision for linking Birmingham city centre with the coalfields of the Black Country was realised. Bypassing the frustratingly slow and expensive delivery by horses on unreliable roads, the canal offered the brass, iron, and tool makers of Birmingham access to cheap and efficiently delivered consignments. The price of coal plummeted, and the Black County had a shot in the arm with a direct link to a hungry market. The extent of the network joining Wolverhampton and the eastern part of the Black Country to Birmingham to the south eventually grew to 174 miles of navigable water[8]. By the nineteenth century, the Black Country had become known as the 'workshop of the world', with the region's products being exported to every corner of the globe.

---

6 There is some dispute over the exact geographical coverage of the Black Country. I favour the interpretation that it is defined by the extent of the black coal field centred on the towns of Walsall, West Bromwich, Dudley, and the City of Wolverhampton.

7 More properly, Thomas Newcomen's atmospheric engine was built in the Black Country in 1712.

8 Comparison is frequently drawn to Venice which has a modest twenty-six miles of canal. A more meaningful comparison would be the entire Norfolk broads which has 120 miles of navigable waterways.

At its height, the sheer scale and intensity of industrial activity in this area was captured in a famous description of the landscape being 'black by day and red by night'[9]. It was not just mass production, there was a rich diversity of products, and certain towns became associated with world-class excellence in certain items. Brierley, for instance, boasted fine-cut glass crystal while Walsall had a thriving leather trade that included luxury items; it was also where the world's first readymade riding saddle was produced[10].

It is tempting to romanticise the period as a golden age where the country prospered, and solid working-class people were able to earn an honest living. The reality was that, for the majority, times were hard and life was a grind. Indentured workers were, in some cases, little better than slave labour. There was a poor standard of housing and dangerous working conditions, where hours were long, and men, women and even children were mercilessly exploited. In addition, a toxic combination of coal mines, iron foundries, glass factories, brickworks, and steel mills made for high levels of air pollution, leading to illness and shortened life expectancies. The grimy landscape itself was scarred by abandoned mines that had become exhausted or unprofitable. The unsightliness of the landscape led the author J. R.R. Tolkien, who lived in nearby Birmingham, to include a fictional place called Mordor in his books. Mordor was a black land, a place of shadows. Legend has it that the curtains on Queen Victoria's rail carriage were closed while the train passed through the area. The eyes of a blue blood royal were averted from the endeavour of blue-collar existence. Heaven forbid that the Queen's eyes should be sullied by the sight of where her people laboured, loved, and lived.

---

9  These colours have more recently been incorporated into the Black Country logo.

10  Thomas Newton produced the world's first readymade riding saddle in Walsall in the 1830s.

By the time the Victorian period ended in 1901, canals were less significant. The development of road and rail produced an improved transport infrastructure, and the whole region was connected by public transport. In addition, individuals found the liberation of increased mobility through bicycles, while the few motor cars that were about were the preserve of rich enthusiasts. Telephones were still in their infancy and gas-powered lighting dominated.

One feature of the Black Country was the growth of workers' dwellings quite close to factories, meaning that housing and industry coexisted cheek by jowl. The few thousand dwellings that grew up on Yew Tree Estate fifty years later were different. West Bromwich County Borough Council had created a modern solution to the housing crisis. This was suburbia, a commuter satellite for the aspirational. Young couples (married, of course), could escape house sharing with in-laws. With hard work to meet monthly mortgage or weekly rent obligations, they could raise 2.4 children together and live happily ever after. At least that was the dream. In the process, children born on the estate escaped a traditional Black Country environment but still became encultured by a shared heritage, sense of humour and dialect. Within this diaspora, there was a coming together of two tribes, Walsall people, and West Bromwich people. Some looked towards Walsall town centre when planning a shopping trip, while others favoured equidistant West Bromwich. Ours was a Walsall household, and the delivery of the broadsheet-sized weekly newspaper, the 'Walsall Observer', on Fridays confirmed as much.

By the time of my birth in 1956, the Black Country was coming to terms with deindustrialisation while starting to shake off some of its industrial blackness. The passing of the Clean Air Act in the same year forced the use of smokeless sources of heat and energy. Coal as a pollutant may have declined, but now there were petrol and diesel exhaust fumes to contend with thanks to the growth in ownership of far from green motorcars and motorcycles. Across the country large-scale building projects were underway to replace the half a million homes destroyed by German bombing during the War. Then there was the cramped back-to-back housing to deal with. One MP bluntly described them as 'lice ridden: rat ridden lost hell holes'[11].

Home ownership was increasing, and although an average house price of £1,891 may seem modest by today's prices, it should be set alongside the fact that an average worker took home a mere ten pounds a week. On the outskirts of towns, brand new estates, such as Yew Tree, sprung up. My house, like many on the estate, was a modest semi-detached redbrick building. I was blindsided to the harshness of the unimaginative uniform houses facing one another, but it was for its time a good, modern home with three bedrooms, gas, and electricity. In a class-conscious society, the professional classes raised the deposit required and committed to monthly mortgage payments to set up a home they could call their own. On the other side of the estate, manual workers stumped up the council rent every week for new semi-detached municipal homes. Housing solutions of the period also included high-rise flats and prefabricated houses (prefabs).

My Estate incorporated what proved to be a short-lived experiment in multi-storey housing. I had a school friend who lived in two-storey Bermuda Mansions, which was neither a piece of a Caribbean paradise nor was it a mansion. There were also a few high-rise blocks (overhyped as 'palaces in the sky'). One spectacular example towered threateningly over the nearby school. It was an ugly pink and grey structure and gloried under the name of 'Churchill Towers'. The building gave all the appearance of an East European architect's idea of combining psychedelia with functionality while using giant Lego blocks.

Mom's parents lived in a bungalow-style prefab a short walk away across the Common. It was a place I visited many times.

_______________________

11 Bessie Braddock, a Liverpool MP, when making her maiden speech in 1945.

The popularity of prefabs lay in the fact that they were a swift and effective solution to the housing crisis. The standard sections for each dwelling could be mass-produced off-site, and once delivered assembly could take place with as little as forty hours of labour. Some of the earliest builds used the labour of German prisoners of war. Ironically, for captured air crews this also meant some reparation for the damage they had caused. Nan and Grandad's single-storey prefab had an indoor toilet and a purpose-built bathroom, which were improvements on their previous dwelling. There must have been twenty or so pre-fabs grouped into two small cul-de-sacs, and my grandparents had the home nearest the road. They now had hot water, an electric fire, insulated floors and roof, and a small garden. Grandad resolutely ignored the garden except for growing some rhubarb under an old metal bucket and putting the dog outside when the need arose. I now know that the pre-fab's insulation was problematic, as it included the now-banned substance asbestos, which could not have helped Nan's long-term lung and breathing problems. Despite this, Nan lived into her nineties.

Yew Tree Estate offered dreamy street names, solid housing, street lighting, a GP surgery, two primary schools[12], and a Walsall postal address. For those who could afford a telephone landline, a unique four-digit number was allocated. Households paid their council rates (taxes) to West Bromwich and had the opportunity to vote for their choice of parliamentary candidate to represent West Bromwich East. The new build estate offered residents an opportunity to forge their own society. The main downside was most evident on hot summer afternoons when the wind was in a certain direction as the smell of Bescot sewerage works two miles away drifted over the estate. There is no place like home. There was no place like my home.

---

12 Consistent with the Estate's naming policy the schools were Yew Tree junior and infant school and Fir Tree junior and infant school.

# Chapter Two

## *Washerwomen and home births*

The middle of the twentieth century was a particularly neurotic time. The most powerful nations on earth were in a tussle to reshape life in the aftermath of a brutal world war. The ideological differences between both sides meant that world politics became reduced to a dangerous board game. You needed to mobilise and then retain support for 'your' ideas as you faced an opponent whose power and support you wished to undermine. On one side of the board were the Americans and their allies representing the West, capitalism , and the rights of the individual. On the other side, Soviet Russia and its allies representing the East and promoting communism, including a controlled economy and collectivism. The game was called the Cold War, and any rules that appeared to be in place were there to be broken. The end game was winning at almost any cost. Both sides used precious resources, ingenuity, and technology to produce better and more powerful weaponry. Then there was a need for espionage to see what the other side was up to. Missiles were in the main unused but threateningly stockpiled. The message was that here was the capability of obliterating whole populations and environments. The underlying belief was that a fragile peace could only be achieved through the destructive power each party held. Triggering a nuclear strike by one side would bring swift retaliation and what became known as MAD 'mutually assured destruction'. MAD became a fitting title for the game that was being played.

Significant in the West/East power game was Egypt. Strategically and geographically, it represented a neutral area in the Middle East. Egypt had once been a mighty nation and had survived and prospered over time as far back as ancient times, not so much due to its alliances with others but due to its biggest natural resource, the river Nile. The Nile has been described as the bread-basket of the nation, compensating for the chronic lack of rainfall with annual floods that produce fertile agricultural land. It is impossible to overstate the significance of the Nile. Some Egyptians view it as sacred and the lifeblood of the country. Ancient historians revered it, believing that the country itself was a gift of the Nile. As far back as 8,000 years ago the river enabled farming to take place along its banks. Centres of civilization grew over time around the Nile Delta. In a valley extending 4,000 miles through a country deprived of rainfall the Nile had represented the country's only source of water. The annual floods irrigated the land, which was enriched by the rich dark waters, ensuring vital crops were possible. In addition, the mighty river offered fish as a source of food and a ready-made waterway as a source of transport. Materials and labour were transported by water to build pyramids and other impressive structures evocative of the powerful ancient Egyptian culture. If this was not enough, reeds growing naturally alongside the river were utilised as materials to build boats and produce papyrus, an early writing material.

Every asset needs investment from time to time, and the Nile was no different. In January 1956, the Egyptian president Gamal Abdel Nasser believed he had funding in place to do just that. Britain, hanging onto the coat tails of America, agreed to jointly provide the significant funds needed to help build a huge dam at Aswan. The project meant that for the first-time annual floods and consequent irrigation of the land could be controlled. Enormous amounts of hydroelectric power could also be generated. Furthermore, navigation routes through the mighty river would be enhanced. The vision, once realised, would produce enormous benefits and completely revitalise Egypt's economy. This was going to be significant.

Several degrees cooler and 4,000 miles away, Councillor Perry was for once absent for the meeting of West Bromwich Council's

General Purposes Committee. He was elsewhere. The reason was that his first child, Robert, was being born in the back bedroom of number 26 Lilac Avenue, Yew Tree Estate, at 4.15 p.m. one January afternoon. Home births of this period were the norm. I am pretty sure that Dad was not in the same room at the time – this was not really the territory for men, even if it was happening in the next room. Along with the midwife who arrived in time by cycling there, Mrs Skinner from next door but one was also in attendance to support Mom. So, I became a first-generation NHS baby. My birth was announced in both the *Walsall Observer* and the *Midland Chronicle*. The town's Mayor (on headed notepaper proudly proclaiming 'telephone West Bromwich 0721, 10 lines') offered warm congratulations on behalf of members to Councillor and Mrs Perry.

Winter gave way to spring and by the July summertime came along. I was just another healthy baby on the Yew Tree estate, experiencing new things from the comfort of a substantial pram. Things like new faces peering into the pram, bright sunshine, and fresh air dependent upon the operations at Bescot sewerage works and the wind direction. My development was going well and the nice young couple at number 26 now had their own family.

Meanwhile, in Egypt matters had taken an unexpected turn. Elements within the US administration had become distrustful of Egypt's supposed dalliances with the Soviet Union and had decided to withdraw their support. This about-face put the UK in a difficult position. The government had no reason to alienate the Egyptian government but, as a very junior partner in the Western alliance, it felt a need to fall in line. Besides, it could not afford to cover the funding itself. Britain followed the US lead.

The scheme was too important to shelve, so Nasser devised a plan B. The busy Suez Canal ran through Egypt. An important route, its 101 miles linked the Indian Ocean and Mediterranean Sea and allowed easier travel between Europe and Asia without going around Africa. Declaring martial law in the area, Nasser seized control of the Suez Canal Company and its canal, calculating that the tolls collected would help finance the building of the dam. The canal carried, amongst other things, vital shipments of oil to Western Europe and significantly was, up until this point, controlled by French and ... British interests. When the canal was dug in 1869, Britain initially opposed its construction. Not because it had been dug by forced labour, but because of the impact it would have on its established trade routes. Then the opportunity for investment came along, which was seized upon. Now there was a major problem.

With diplomatic efforts to settle the crisis faltering, Britain and France prepared for military action to regain control of the canal and, if possible, remove Nasser as leader. Interests and a supply of oil to Europe via the canal were all important. In October 1956, an initial bombing exercise was followed by British troops joining with invading French and Israeli forces hoping to reclaim the canal. The initiative was roundly condemned both at home and amongst the international community, with many claiming the actions to be 'illegal'. Even the superpowers, the United States and the Soviet Union, for once had an issue they could agree on. The 'Suez crisis' was in full swing, and the world held its breath. The Soviets seized the opportunity of a distracted West to invade Hungary and reassert Soviet rule. (A student-led protest in Budapest had sparked a nationwide uprising against the Hungarian rulers and Soviet-imposed policies.)

The British government's belief in the justification for a military build-up was not shared by opposition parties. On 4th. November a major demonstration through London was organised by the Labour Party under the banner of 'Law Not War'. Labour councillors in West Bromwich decided to make their protest by walking out of the next council meeting after a few minutes. There was, however, one dissenting voice within the Labour ranks. Cllr Donald Perry strongly disagreed with the action, making clear he would take no part. (I am not sure whether he thought the action too trivial and futile or whether he supported the Government's handling of the crisis.)

The warmth and goodwill extended to Don Perry a few months earlier was in short supply when the town's weekly newspaper hit the local newsstands. It was reported on the front cover that Cllr Perry felt that his colleagues were acting like 'a bunch of washer women'. I am not sure how washer women act, but I am pretty sure that by today's standards the comment would be decried as sexist. What I am sure of is that it was not meant as a complimentary term.

In the absence of wider significant international support, with the Americans against the actions and with the country split on the issue, a humiliating withdrawal took place in early 1957. The Suez affair had a lasting significance. Britain's lack of political and military muscle was laid bare, something that needed acknowledging and coming to terms with. Prime Minister Sir Anthony Eden resigned, humiliated, in January 1957. The ruling Conservative party rang the changes in their own way. Eden (ex-Eton College and Oxford University) was replaced by Harold Macmillan (ex-Eton College and Oxford University). For the US, relations with the Middle East were significantly damaged and would take decades of diplomacy to repair. Egypt now had in Nasser a hero who had stood up to and defeated the bullying ambitions of Britain and France, something all other Arab nations applauded.

The dam itself was finally completed in 1970. Its huge main reservoir, which was the third largest in the world, was named Lake Nasser. Nasser died the same year as the dam's completion, and there was a genuine outpouring of grief across the whole Arab world, with five million people paying their respects at his funeral in Cairo. Nasser's courage had meant progress towards social justice, Arab unity, and modernisation of his country. His name would be long remembered, and parents approving of his anti-imperialist stance named their sons after him. The name of Anthony Eden, the Prime Minister responsible for the Suez debacle, would not be remembered in the same way. Little did Eden know that forty-three years after the crisis, England's cricket team would be captained by someone named Nasser Hussain. A final posthumous insult.

# Chapter Three

## *My parents*

Doreen's story

The red brick semi-detached houses stood to attention in two straight lines in Lilac Avenue. The unyielding uniformity of housing screamed out for some individuality. Some of the residents responded by painting their front doors in eye-catching colours. Number 26 had a tangerine-coloured door. Not only that, it also had a curious name. A wooden plaque announced to the world that this house was called DONRODOR. The couple in this home had certain shared dreams and ambitions, some of which they had already realised. Meet someone and settle down, tick. Find a place of your own, tick. Start a family, not yet.

Doreen was a loving person with a keen sense of right and wrong. Born in Palfrey, Walsall in 1931 and raised during the hardship of the Great Depression, a time of extraordinary global economic downturn when there were no safety nets or welfare systems. During her formative years, and with no siblings for company, she saw as highlights 'get togethers' with extended families. These gatherings involved everyone giving a performance, maybe singing, reciting a poem, or clowning about. Doreen learned to play the piano. If these gatherings offered entertainment, then excitement came in the form of spending evenings in the air raid shelter at the bottom of her Gran's garden during bombing raids between 1940 and 1944. Thousands of Anderson air raid shelters were issued free to poorer families such as Doreen's[13]. Walsall was an obvious target as the variety and volume of its manufactured products were vital to

---

13 Any family earning less than £250 a year or approximately £16,500 today.

the war effort. Although the town did suffer some bomb damage it thankfully escaped quite lightly. The nearest it came to widespread damage was when the German Luftwaffe dropped a bomb on Pleck gas works, one and a half miles away from where Doreen lived. Thankfully the bomb failed to explode.

Doreen, like many of her peers, left school aged fourteen so that she could start work and bring some money into the house. She got a job in the office of a garage in Walsall. As she got older, she began going to local dances with her friends and, at one, met her future husband, who was on leave from the army. The war was ending while Donald (who was six years her senior) was completing his training with the Royal Engineers at Pickering, North Yorkshire. Soon he found himself stationed in Klagenfurt, Austria, as part of a peacekeeping and reconstruction effort. In an era predating email, mobiles and social media communication was difficult and far from instantaneous. Nevertheless, a daily routine of writing inky letters and posting them to one another followed. Naturally, responses in a time-lapsed fashion made for fractured conversations, but despite this, the long-distance romance thrived.

At the time food and sweets were still rationed. Doreen's father suggested that as they were already saving the money and ration coupons to enable her to enjoy a good coming-of-age birthday celebration, she might as well get married. It may not have been romantic, but it was practical. So it was that Doreen proposed to Don, not even face to face but by letter. She had to wait for a return post some days later before getting the answer 'yes, yes, yes, yes, yes' written on a single sheet of note paper[14].

The marriage took place on Doreen's twenty-first birthday at St. John's Church of England church in the Pleck, just along from the gas works that had miraculously survived during the war. There were several challenges in staging the event

---

14  As their son I cannot consider the possibility that this was in a 'Harry met Sally' way.

successfully. First there was the concerted endeavour required to collect  enough food ration tokens to put on a decent spread. Then there were the last-minute changes to the flowers for the bouquet. The wedding date happened to fall the day after the funeral of King George VI, and Mom's choice of red roses for her big day was frustrated as florists had redirected all available stems to St. George's Chapel on the Windsor Castle estate[15]. Then there was the biting cold February weather which made it uncomfortable hanging about for photographs. Everything, despite these challenges, seemed to be going well until, as the day wore on, it became evident to Doreen that her new husband had not bought her either a present or card to mark her milestone birthday. He had simply forgotten or not bothered. He would be reminded of this oversight several times over the fifty-five years of marriage that followed. Many men would be embarrassed by such a blunder or attempt to rectify it afterward. Donald was not one of those men.

Early married life together involved the challenge of doing as most married couples of the period did, living in the same home as their parents while waiting for a council house 'to come up'. (Once married, couples would apply for a council house and then join a lengthy waiting list.) Doreen's parents lived in a small, pre-fabricated house, so it meant sharing a home with Don's family, which included a father-in-law and two sisters-in-law, one with a husband and young children.

One Sunday afternoon the newlyweds paid a visit to Doreen's parents and offered to take the dog for a walk. They had not gone far when they saw that construction work was going on just the other side of Delves Common. The start of a housing estate. If

---

15 Following the death of her father George, from lung cancer, Queen Elizabeth II had her Coronation sixteen months later. She went on to become the country's longest serving monarch ever.

only they could save the deposit, they could get a mortgage and get a place of their own. This was a shared dream that became a reality, and they became the first residents of number 26 Lilac Avenue on a fledgling estate in 1953.

They determined to start a family. More than that, they would first have a boy whose name was going to be Robert. This was a time when anything seemed possible, and so confident were they that their plans would come to fruition that they hung a sign bearing the name DONRODOR (a Donald, Robert, Doreen combination) over the front door. Every time they walked through the door it was there as a reminder of the next stage on their shared life plan. It must have been a terrible blow when Doreen had a miscarriage in 1954. Now things were going according to plan once more, and the National Health Service (NHS) would help remove the worry of a problematic birth.

Some think it curious that Winston Churchill led the country through a world war, but he and his party were then rejected at the first election in peacetime. The reason was that the opposition Labour Party had the most convincing vision for a much-needed reconstruction of the country. The new government's vision embraced extensive nationalisation[16] and the creation of the NHS. By the time I was born the service was still bedding in after its earlier introduction by the then Health Secretary, Nye Bevan on 5 July 1948. The government heralded the service as the 'envy of the world' at a time when few countries had or even dreamt of a universal health system. The scheme involved drawing together the work of hospitals, pharmacists, opticians, and dentists into a

---

16 Nationalisation included the Bank of England, railways and the coal, gas, and the electricity industries. The US administration were appalled by such socialist policies and called in its considerable war time debts, so creating a financial pinch that necessitated the need for rationing to continue into the 1950s.

unified service. The radical change was that these services were provided free at the point of delivery to everyone 'from cradle to grave'. Although derided by its opponents, it proved in time to be successful and popular, a jewel in the crown of Clement Attlee's Labour Government. Much later, marking seventy years of service, the Guardian described it as 'an institution that is not just the country's most vital public service but also an embodiment of an inspiring set of shared values ... civilised, compassionate Britain in action, 24/7'.

Don's story

So here he was, Donald Perry, the proud owner of 26 Lilac Avenue. (Technically he faced 25 years of mortgage repayments to *Walsall Mutual Building Society* before he owned it legally.) He had overcome adversity to get his own piece of normality. No longer just a son and brother, he was a husband and now a father. Things were on the up.

Born in Sedgley, but raised in Walsall, Don was an entirely different kettle of fish to his wife Doreen. His early life was rather different to hers. His downtrodden mother died when he was only fourteen years old. His father, Job, was a hardworking, hard-drinking veteran of the First World War who had little interest in family life and offered little in the way of praise or encouragement to his three children. Don's older sister, Daisy, who was named after her mother, took on the vacated maternal role by caring for her younger siblings. She was a kindly, unassuming sort who suffered with her nerves.

So, the teenage Don shared a family home with his wayward father, a sometimes difficult younger sister, Margaret, the long-suffering Daisy, as well as Len, Daisy's husband, and their young children Roy and Pat. He was keen to swap this life for another and volunteered for the armed forces as soon as he could and before he was conscripted. This turned out to be a masterstroke, as he found himself a new home and a life he loved. The forces offered him new experiences, travel overseas, and, more importantly, structure, purpose, and the potential for self-development. Fellow soldiers as conscripts were slightly poorer paid than volunteers. Repeated jibes of 'regular soldier, regular bastard' were water off a duck's back to Don. He had found a place of belonging. Seizing the opportunities available, he trained and qualified as a draughtsman with an engineering background and earned his stripes to become a sergeant. He probably would have signed on for a further term in the army had it not been for meeting Doreen and that letter.

After being demobbed into civvy street, he soon found employment in a draughtsman office in Birmingham. By now he was married and had a steady job that did not involve the hard manual labour in a Walsall steel works or factory that his former school friends faced. The big problem was that he was back at the Perry family home, with its limited privacy and pleasure. He was back at a place he had managed to escape once by joining the army. This time it was with his new bride. The solution to his problem took the form of a move to a new estate on the other side of town. This was not any house either. This was a brand-new home with modern facilities, the sort that estate agents of the period referred to as a 'des res' – a desirable residence. His new neighbours were of a similar age, newly married and with working careers and dreams and aspirations of their own. This new estate was a place to fit in and contribute to a society that was being created.

As a trade union activist and branch secretary, Don took his responsibilities very seriously and was diligent and well respected. He made his biggest mark by lobbying the local MP to bring forward a private member's bill protecting office and shop workers and improving their working conditions. His letter outlining the case was quoted verbatim in the Commons and is recorded in Hansard for all time. The Labour Party had grown out of the trade union movement, and he enjoyed the rough and tumble of political involvement and arguments with not only bosses in his union role but also others within the same Party over questions of policy. He was selected as a candidate for the local elections, ran a successful campaign, and became an elected member of West Bromwich Council a year before the first of his children was born. His son came along, but the demands of being both a union branch secretary and local councillor continued.

One Tuesday evening after he had finished work, he did not have time to go home, so went straight to a hall in West Bromwich for a union meeting. As his, like most houses, did not have a landline, he was unable to phone Doreen to make sure that everything was all right. He had however warned her that he would be home late. At the meeting he was soon on his feet contesting some issue as unconstitutional and ended up in a fulsome debate with someone who happened to be a communist. Harsh words were said on both sides, but to show there were no hard feelings he bought his opponent a pint in the bar afterwards. Then, still cradling his glass of flat, keg dispensed apology for beer he networked with a few of the lads from other branches in an atmosphere thick with cigarette smoke and intrigue. The union letters and circulars he was carrying around in his briefcase would have to be dealt with tomorrow if he could juggle that around all the paperwork he had to go through before the Council meeting later that week. As he travelled home, he reflected on the labels he had acquired. A family man, a valued professional with a steady job, an effective trade unionist and an outspoken member of the local council. Now he had respect and status, and ambitions for more things besides.

During the fifties, trade union membership and its muscle was growing significantly. Today, union membership has fallen back to around six million people. Then it was around nine million and on a steep incline before peaking a few decades later at twelve million[17]. In the 1950s, union muscle was necessary to

---

17 Then came the intervention of a Thatcher led Conservative government during the 1980s.

counter the arcane management practices at some firms. The year I was born unions led 6,000 car workers through a six-week strike in response to the sacking of workers without consultation or notice. This was sixteen short miles away at Longbridge, and there must have been people from the estate involved. The year following there were national strikes in both shipbuilding and engineering.

The 1959 BAFTA-winning Ealing studio comedy *I'm All Right Jack,* starring Peter Sellers, parodied the poor state of British industrial relations at the time as well as underlining the power of unions. The sixties and seventies saw unprecedented levels of industrial action being taken. Factory workers and others were not to be treated as an expendable source of production, or as malevolent automatons. Industrial disputes were legion, with strikes, both official and unofficial, occurring at the drop of a cloth cap or was it at the drop of another management clanger? Most probably, it was some combination.

Many union leaders featured regularly on newspaper front pages and were better known than most MPs. Government policy at the time was formulated recognising the unions as a legitimate representative of one of the factors of production during the sixties. Under Harold Wilson's Labour government, visits by trade union leaders to join Downing Street discussions attracted the unflattering tag of 'beer and sandwiches' meetings by the press. The link between trade unions and the Labour Party remained strong and union involvement was a legitimate and well-trodden route to becoming a Labour MP. It had been suggested to Don that he might want to consider letting his name go forward to join a short list of candidates to replace a retiring Labour MP in the northeast.

Lilac Avenue was dimly lit by the streetlamps as Don made his way home. He was tired but stimulated by the day's events. He was nearly home and there might be some supper in the offing, there was normally. Tonight, there was something else waiting for him besides, something he had not bargained for. As he opened the front door, he found Doreen sitting there alone while the baby slept upstairs. It was time for a few home truths. She was just getting over her second miscarriage and needed a bit of help. She had not seen anyone all day, the twin tub washing machine was playing up, and the baby had cried most of the early evening. It was time to spell out the obvious. He now had family responsibilities. He engaged in far too much out of the house. He was never there in the week. It was time to recalibrate their relationship and Donald's input to home life. Something would have to give. The easiest was the Council, which was a bloody nuisance what with all the meetings and all the stuff that came through the post for him to read.

This was a hammer blow for Don. For once the plain talking came from someone else. He listened and acknowledged the logic even if he felt it necessary to put up some sort of lame argument. Doreen was right, and grumpily, he made the necessary adjustments.

Did he look in on me asleep in my room that night? Did he see a sleeping baby and think giving up party political involvement was a small price to pay? Alternatively, did he think this sleeping baby is the stumbling block to achieving my political ambitions?

He may have lost his involvement, but never lost his interest in politics. Had he ever been on the TV Quiz programme *Mastermind*, then his specialist subject would certainly have been parliamentary constituencies and their MPs. He could name the parliamentary constituencies and the approximate majorities enjoyed by MPs. He also offered sometimes startling commentary whether you wanted to hear it or not. This was some party trick that he enacted at every opportunity, even when not invited to do so.

'South Worcestershire? That is Gerald Nabbaro, he used to represent Kidderminster, a 5,000 majority, it's been Tory for years. He has a huge moustache and a car with a NAB registration. What a complete burke he is!'

'George Brown? Belper in Derbyshire, 8,000 Labour majority. He likes his drink, and he needs a good haircut.'

'Of course, Wolverhampton South West is Enoch Powell's constituency, brilliant intellect. Heath hates him, of course; it could go either way in the next election.'

'Did you say Leeds? Well, Denis Healy represents Leeds East. He has a 5,000 majority but needs his eyebrows sorting out.'

He would have cleaned up on *Mastermind*, and his enthusiasm and encyclopaedic knowledge would have served him well had he become an MP himself. Not that he would have been offered a cabinet post. Instead, he would have been a maverick back bench MP and a nightmare for the whips wanting him to toe the party line. If only ...

# WORLD EVENTS

# Chapter Four

## *News of the world*

The saying 'May you live in interesting times' may be as genuinely Chinese as the children's game Chinese whispers. In other words, not Chinese at all. Whatever the origin of the phrase, the words might be taken as a blessing while hinting at something darker. The saying could have been devised for the time I was born. Everyone's upbringing is locked into a particular place and time, and mine is no exception. This was an interesting period of history, not just because of newsworthy events but thanks to an undeniable undercurrent of the threat of yet another conflict over the Suez crisis and, of course, the ongoing Cold War.

Nowadays individuals do not so much seek the news as be bombarded by it. Aside from the newspapers in print and digital form, there is rolling television coverage on several channels. Then there is a vast choice of digital radio stations, some solely dedicated to news coverage. Meanwhile everyday life is interrupted by mobile devices bringing news flashes and breaking stories. The internet contains a legion of sites jostling with one another to bring news. Newsworthy happenings, some filmed on mobile devices, can take the viewer to unfolding events in real time, complete with running commentary and analysis. News has become instant rather than the delay involved in relying on the reports of 'correspondents' some time afterwards. Sharing of images and soundbites on social media draws further comments and reposts. Increasingly a younger generation prefers social media as their prime source of news[18]. Whatever form it takes, news is inescapable.

---

18 Worryingly 'fake news' peddles mistruths or part truths so shaping and cementing attitudes and beliefs in a particular way.

How different it all seemed when I was young. Not that news was viewed as being unimportant then, far from it. Indeed, news seemed vital to both my parents. Mom and Dad made deliberate attempts to acquire it. They paid for the privilege of having newspapers delivered to the house. There was *The Birmingham Post* six mornings a week ('a good mix of national and local coverage' according to Dad), *The Sunday Telegraph* (the distinct Tory viewpoint making it a curious choice for a Labour voting household) and every Friday, the *Walsall Observer*. All three publications were broadsheet size, contained black and white photography and left print on the hands.

The *Walsall Observer* was a composite of local happenings, stories of court cases, photographs of buildings getting opened, decisions of the council, things the town's MPs had been involved in and planning objections. Listings of births, marriages, and deaths assumed far greater significance than the advertisements that dominate today's local newspapers. Although the announcement in the local papers of the birth of her first grandchild was a source of pride for Nan, she was, as a rule, more interested in the alphabetic listing of the recently deceased. Her Friday morning routine involved a mug of tea and the careful scanning of the relevant newspaper column.

My father-in-law spent his entire working life in the newspaper industry. I know from him that even into the 1980s the industry was more reliant on mechanisation than computerisation. Laborious production processes involved the use of toxic ink, acid, painstaking type setting and careful proofreading. With such time-consuming systems, daily newspapers were, by necessity, reporting what had happened the day before while hinting at unfolding events. Once on sale, newsagent shops and street corner vendors in towns were equipped with a caged billboard, which encouraged would-be buyers with eye-catching headlines. These could range from the highly significant, such as 'National crisis latest', to the more trivial, in the case of the local press, such as 'sneak thieves steal washing off line'.

As well as print, radio and television were valued additional news sources. Growing up, adults were either watching or listening to the news or waiting for it to be broadcast.

'… the news will be on in a minute …'
  '… we will do it after the news …'
  '… I will just make a pot of tea, then the news will be on …'
  And so on.

The experience of having gathered around 'wireless' radio sets during the war to get important, grave, and life-changing announcements inevitably shaped my parents' thinking. This was the generation that had something hardwired into their DNA that made them thirsty for news updates, preferably from the government's own British Broadcasting Corporation (BBC). Now, in a different decade, they were still listening for news that might be significant. They needed to be told of an 'inevitable' launch of a Soviet missile or of an unfolding nuclear Armageddon.

Although the family television set was always there, it is the music and rhythmic phrases of radio that have ingrained my memories most deeply. Mostly they involved unlikely broadcasts. For instance, the shipping forecast. I never listened to what was being said, but the plummy tones stuck with me. The relevance of the broadcast to a child who lived about as far from the sea as anywhere you can get in this country is not great. I did however relish hearing the familiar voice reciting phrases like '… *Dogger, Fisher, German Bight, moderate* …' Strange words conveying a message of obvious importance that I did not understand, words that needed reciting in a certain sequence like a set prayer. Then there was the rousing opening music announcing it was Saturday and 'This is Sports Report.' This was good marching music for a young child and his kid brother, as was the music introducing another deceptively boring episode of *The Archers*, 'an everyday tale of country folk,' (… dum-dee dum-dee dum-dee dum …). Still going strong, *The Archers* may no longer be the everyday tale it once was. Having first aired nationally in 1951, this is unsurprising. The programme represents the world's longest-running drama. Radio provided a regular repetition of music and phrases, offering comfort in their familiarity, a message that everything was normal, that it was life as usual. Then there was the news update. Brother Tim and I would get a distinctive digest as our parents discussed the significant issues of the day. Neither party was reticent in forcefully giving their personal viewpoint.

'I think it's disgusting,' (Mom),
    'Well, all this is because his problem is ...' (Dad),
    'It's like these berks I have to deal with at work, I told them quite bluntly ...' (Dad),
    and so on.

Our house was more than a place where four people co-existed. It was a home, and a focal point was the dining table. Here, topics of the day would be chewed over along with the food. Sometimes Dad would be so enraged by a news item that he would turn red and shout as he spelt out his own distinctive take on matters. Other times, a story would provoke outrageous comments or have him entering cul-de-sacs on tangential subjects. Happenings on the estate, in the school and in Dad's world of work would also be shared. Like all pre-teenage kids, I carried the imprint of my parents, their preferences, attitudes, values, and biases. Some cultures venerate the older generation. Others tolerate them. In my culture, most children look to adults for answers. Along the way they fail to notice their mistakes and contradictions until they become teenagers. Dad, being outspoken and having a distinctive take on most matters was tolerated because that was part of how he was. When I hit my teenage years, I began questioning and challenging his viewpoints.

The more newsworthy events of the time give a flavour of the world in which I was born. This was the year that Premium savings bonds were launched on behalf of the government. For those with an interest in British history, however, the year 1956 will forever be linked with the word 'crisis' rather than financial prudence. The 'Suez crisis' and the Cold War are dealt with elsewhere. The entire period was lived under the dark cloud of two quarrelling Cold War giants, the United States and Russia and the Soviet Union. Once wartime allies, there were several low points in relations between the two, including one in 1956 when the Russians brutally suppressed an uprising in a neighbouring country. Any one of a series of incidents, including this one, could easily have triggered a war that would inevitably have involved the use of nuclear weapons.

Joe Stalin had led the Soviet Union for twenty-six years until his death in 1953 and was succeeded by Nikita Khrushchev. In February 1956, Khrushchev denounced a 'Stalin' personality cult that had grown up and criticised his running of the Union. Emboldened by such comments, Hungarians began to protest against their pro-Stalinist leadership. Issues of Soviet occupation, food shortages and a lack of liberty were daringly put on the agenda. The authorities were not impressed, and the tension was palpable. The Hungarian people needed help, but the West feared the consequences of any intervention. That same year the Summer Olympics was in Melbourne, and by chance Hungary and the Soviets were pitched against one another in a game of water polo. The Olympic spirit was set aside as the match degenerated into such a violent affair that it became known as 'the blood in the water match'. Back in Hungary, Soviet troops restored order, and an uprising was violently crushed on 4 November 1956. Three thousand Hungarians died in the process, and 200,000 fled abroad as refugees.

It is perhaps of some significance that this was the year that a memorial to Karl Marx was unveiled at his grave at Highgate Cemetery in north London. The political thinker's publications[19]

---

19 Most notably the 1848 pamphlet The Communist Manifesto and the
   four-volume Das Kapital (1867–1883).

had shaped the future political direction of many of the countries that now held diametrically opposed views to those held by my own country.

The power of nuclear energy was first demonstrated in August 1945, when the United States used atomic bombs to bring an earlier end to the Second World War[20]. The States may have been the first nation to develop nuclear weapons, but now their rivals had a similar capability. Britain determined to develop its own nuclear capability and tested its first bomb in the early 1950s. Britain's interest also extended to nuclear energy, and 1956 saw the first commercial station officially opened by a young Queen Elizabeth II in Sellafield, Cumbria. The site became the focus for the country's nuclear industry, both military and energy.

Cold War rivals the United States and the Soviet Union had announced their intention to get an artificial satellite into space the year earlier. By 1956 the Soviets were well advanced with their plans to launch Sputnik 1, which they did the following year. This demonstration of technological superiority shocked the Americans, who suspected that their arch-rivals would use space as a platform to launch missiles. The Space Race was well and truly underway, with each advance used as a propaganda point-scoring exercise.

As the Cold War blew, a new world was emerging. The Suez debacle had irreparably damaged the country's international reputation and finally confirmed the end of Britain as a world force. The British Empire, for better or worse, was fast becoming a chapter of history that had now long passed, signalled most prominently by India gaining independence nine years earlier. School atlases might continue to show a third of the countries coloured pink, but it was fooling no one. In addition, the country

---

20 The Japanese cities of Hiroshima and Nagasaki were targeted.

was burdened by crippling debts, a legacy of fighting the Second World War. It was easily apparent that politically the country would need to come to terms with a new world order where it was no longer a major player.

Western civilisation had benefitted economically, culturally, and socially from colonialism, but change was happening. In Africa, countries including Sudan, Tunisia and Morocco gained independence. In Asia, Pakistan became the first Islamic republic in the world.

Meanwhile, China, a country of 612 million people, had its own version of communism following a recent victory in a civil war led by Chairman Mao. Mao's reign proved to be a brutal experience, and not just for intellectuals and dissidents. During the fifties, Mao enforced a central plan to transform the country's agricultural economy into an industrial one. The transition proved to be too rapid, however, and food shortages claimed the lives of anything between fifteen and fifty-five million Chinese peasants over a four-year period. Today, China has become the world's largest manufacturer and exporter. The cost of the journey to reach that position was paid in the fifties and was tragically much too heavy.

On a lighter note, 1956 was a significant year for popular music. This was the year that rock and roll music exploded, and it was singer Elvis Presley who lit the fuse. In January, shortly after his twenty-first birthday, singer Presley made his first appearance on American television promoting the record *Heartbreak Hotel*. Some viewers saw Elvis ('the pelvis') as a threat to public decency due to his supposedly sexually provocative movements. His unique brand of music and persona bewitched others. More TV appearances followed that year, setting records for viewing figures. Later appearances were wisely filmed from the waist upwards. For the next two years, Elvis dominated the bestselling record charts and was at the forefront of rock and roll music.

Bruce Springsteen saw the first TV performance as a child and was highly influenced by what he saw, commenting later that Elvis had 'let the rock and roll genie out of the bottle'. The music of Elvis and his contemporaries inspired aspiring musicians who found fame in the following decade, including *The Beatles* and *The Rolling Stones*. These British bands went on to transform popular music forever. Referred to as the 'King', Presley's style and mix of musical influences opened the door for African American performers to find a wider white audience. The following year his single *Hound Dog* (which had *Don't Be Cruel* on the other side) was his best-selling single ever[21]. Presley went on to achieve chart success not only in the fifties but also in each of the decades that followed up until the 2010s, long after his death. To date, record sales have topped six hundred million worldwide, and Elvis (who died in 1977) is regarded as a cultural icon. Back in the fifties, his manager, Colonel Tom Parker, exploited his popularity to the full, which included many business ventures and the making of several truly awful movies.

About this time another celebrated figure from the world of entertainment was at the height of their power. No one would claim that Marilyn Monroe was a great actress, but what she lacked in acting ability, she more than made up for in presence and raw sex appeal. From Andy Warhol's pop art depiction to the photograph of a laughing on-screen Monroe clinging to her dress in a breeze from a subway vent, it is impossible to shake her image from your memory. Monroe starred in numerous commercially successful films during the fifties, and although her work was straightforward and comfortingly lightweight, her private life was turbulent. She had several lovers, including a US President, was married and divorced three times and died in tragic circumstances in 1962.

---

21 Estimates vary but most compilers agree that this is the case.

While Monroe's films were romantic comedies, the top grossing films of the time included the biblical epic *The Ten Commandments*, the musical *The King and I* and the adventure *Around the World in Eighty Days*. A high point for cinema numbers occurred ten years earlier with 1.6 billion attendances, but by the 1950s, numbers had slipped despite being significant[22]. As cinema had squeezed music hall and theatre attendances, so television was now squeezing cinema.

Our family outings to the cinema were limited to two or three a year, normally coinciding with someone's birthday or being on holiday when the weather was not so good. We normally went armed with boiled sweets or sandwiches wrapped in foil. The films that my parents were drawn to were predictable, with favourites being a 'Carry on' or a James Bond movie. The plots of these films were also predictable. James Bond would battle a master villain while using gadgets, fast cars, and faster girls. The 'Carry on' plots would feature familiar characters in contrived situations culminating in a joke about Barbara Windsor's breasts. Trips to the cinema came complete with an intermission between the B movie (a supporting film) and the main feature. Some films were in black and white and others in glowing *Technicolor*. We once went to see the film *Summer Holiday* and were a little disappointed when the opening black and white scenes came on the screen until the film's star, Cliff Richard, stepped off a double decker bus and the movie changed into full colour. The whole audience in the cinema applauded.

In terms of football, the game I grew to love, 1956 was the year that the first floodlit league match was staged[23]. It was also this year that the inaugural award was made of the prestigious Ballon

---

22  The big drop off came from the 1960s onwards.

23  The match was between Portsmouth and Newcastle on 22 February 1956, there was delay by half an hour because of a fuse failure.

d'Or (Golden Ball) trophy to the player voted by journalists as the best player in Europe. Their choice was Stanley Matthews, then of Blackpool and a spritely forty-one years old. In Brazil, Santos signed a fifteen-year-old boy by the name of Edson Arantes do Nascimento with unimagined success. He went on to serve the club for nineteen seasons, averaged a goal for every game played, smashed all goalscoring records and won three world cups for Brazil. Rightly acknowledged as the greatest player of all time, he was better known as Pele. The domestic game itself had many features that now seem strange. Football at Christmas meant successive fixtures against the same opposition, both home and away, with matches played on both Christmas Day and Boxing Day. Due to the paucity of reporting outlets, supporters often turned up on Boxing Day unaware of the previous day's result. Meanwhile, players were the 'property' of their clubs, unable to seek a living elsewhere under an almost feudal 'retain and keep' system, with pay capped by a League stipulated maximum wage. Supporters could smoke while watching a game. Images of players smoking advertised certain brands of cigarette while other brands used to give away cigarette cards, some featuring a colour picture on the front and information on the player on the rear. This particular year Manchester City won the FA Cup, and reigning League champions Manchester United ignored Football League advice to take part in a fledgling European Cup competition (now the UEFA Champions League). Manager Matt Busby thought his young players would benefit from the experience, and English football had much to learn from Europe. He was right, but tragedy was to strike two years later with the Munich air disaster. A plane carrying the team, supporters, and press crashed on its third attempt to take off from a slush-covered runway at Munich en route from a game in Belgrade. Of the forty-four people on the plane, twenty-three perished.

The West may have looked to America for cultural icons in the form of Elvis and Marilyn Monroe; right-minded people however shunned the country's appalling practice of racial segregation.

December 1956 was a significant date in the struggle for racial equality when, after a year of campaigning, the Supreme Court declared Alabama and Montgomery laws requiring segregated buses illegal.

Sometimes it takes a single issue to spark a wider debate and renewed protests. In 2020, the death of George Floyd while being arrested by police in Minnesota led to the 'Black Lives Matter' campaign. Similarly, a reinvigorated challenge to segregation had been sparked when Rosa Parks, an African American, was arrested for refusing to surrender her seat on a bus to a white person. An effective bus boycott and legal challenge was led by a charismatic Baptist pastor by the name of Martin Luther King Jr. The success in the courtroom may not have ended segregation[24], but it was a seminal victory for the Civil Rights Movement in an ongoing battle.

All this was too much for white supremacists, and an organisation originally founded in 1866, the Ku Klux Klan, found new life ninety years later. The group campaigned for the boycott of black singers and for the removal of rock and roll records from jukeboxes. Though thankfully short-lived, the group left a violent stain on the American conscience. Low points included an on-stage assault of jazz pianist and singer Nat King Cole[25] and orchestrating a riot in Clinton, Tennessee. One atrocity involved ceremonially castrating a man and leaving him for dead at the roadside for the crime of not having the 'right' skin colour.

Across the South Atlantic Ocean, South Africa was exercising its own version of racial segregation. The policy of separating

---

24 White-only restaurants and theatres continued in the southern states and interracial marriage was punishable by law in most states until 1967.

25 Nat King Cole became the first African American entertainer with a network television series when he earned a deal in 1956.

the ruling white minority from the rest was known as apartheid[26] By classifying everyone according to a category of race, all non-whites were prevented from entering white areas. The policy was strengthened by 'pass' laws which required non-whites to carry documents authorising their presence in restricted areas. In August 1956, 20,000 South African women, including Indians, Coloureds, Blacks, and some Whites[27], marched in protest on one of the country's capital cities, Pretoria. The so-called 'Women's March' played a significant role in the anti-apartheid struggle and became a noteworthy moment in women's history.

At that time, Nelson Mandela was a leader in the African National Congress (ANC) Defiance Campaign, involving violating curfews and refusing to carry identification passes. Mandela, along with 8,000 others, was jailed as a result. Continuing to campaign on release, he was tried but found not guilty of treason in 1956. He was later convicted on a separate charge in 1964, leading to twenty-seven years of imprisonment. Unbeknown to him at the time, Mandela became the face of the struggle and the world's best-known political prisoner. Many countries applied political pressure and sanctions against South Africa until a new president, F.W. de Klerk, pledged to end apartheid and release Mandela from prison in 1990.

These stories give a flavour of the world I was born into. The news of the world formed a wallpaper to everyday life on the estate I grew up on. This was a time of certain seismic events like the Suez crisis and the Hungarian uprising. Deep divisions based on political philosophy and skin colour were all too apparent. In the absence of a nuclear war to end all wars, other battles were being fought, including the Cold War, the space race, and

---

26 Apartheid is Afrikaans for 'apartness'.

27 These were the categories that were applied by the South African government.

the battles of the Civil Rights and anti-Apartheid movements. Empires were crumbling and new world powers were emerging. This was a brutal, extreme period of history with an undercurrent of impending mutual annihilation. The world was first introduced to rock and roll. The figures of Nasser, Khrushchev, Mao, Rosa Parks, Mandela, and Elvis strode through it all. Eager audiences devoured key stories and tales of landmark events until radio and television sets were switched off at night and newspapers were consigned to the rubbish bin. Then the pattern was repeated the next day.

May you live in interesting times? There surely was never a boring 'slow news' day in 1956.

# Chapter Five

## *Living under the shadow*

I was too young. I was unaware of the detail of what was happening and incapable of understanding its implications. I did however know that something was happening. Something far away, something to cause deep concern. Some dog owners claim that their pet gets restless before a thunderstorm, knowing something is in the air. I do not claim to possess a similar inane sense of canine intuition. What understanding I gained was straightforwardly gleaned from listening to an adult conversation. What I picked up was that the world, that is the whole of Yew Tree estate and the Delves area of Walsall, plus all the other bits, was under a huge imminent threat. I would die, my family would die, everyone on the estate would die, so would Nan and Grandad. The world would perish.

What began as an unremarkable day at school became the first time that I realised all was not well. What's more, my parents could not sort it out. This was the day that I discovered that grownups do bad things, are fallible, and the mistakes they make can make others feel vulnerable, helpless even. I was at the end of the street holding Mom's hand as she and a gossip of mothers stopped walking to engage in conversation. It was a bitterly cold October day, so hanging around was a strange thing to do. What alerted me to the need to listen was that the conversation would, at certain points, be conducted in hushed tones. Glancing protectively at their offspring voices became muted or turned into off-stage whispers.

'... Well, you know what the Russians are like. Mumble, mumble.'

'... and we all know what that means, ... mumble.'

'... it's no use saying we are not involved. Mumble, mumble.'

I overheard someone utter the words 'the end of the world'. The talking paused momentarily, and there were nods and sad-looking faces. As the conversation reached some sort of conclusion, someone said something profound but frustratingly inaudible and looked heavenwards. Others looked in the same direction. Were they looking at the clouds for falling bombs or towards Bescot sewerage station? I picked up on the gravity of it all and the fear that everyone seemed to share. It seemed obvious that we were all in this together, but there was not much we could do about the situation. For anyone to be safe, we all had to be safe, but how?

After a demoralising walk home, families went their own ways to the pressing priorities of settling down for *Blue Peter*[28] on the television and getting tea underway. Tea and television were all very well, but there were bigger issues to contend with. I may only have been five years old, and here I was part of a world blighted by the threat of nuclear weapons, the fallout from a mutual distrust between two mighty Cold War warriors and of course the stifling fear of ordinary people.

The story of this crisis began to unfold a few years earlier to a time when I was a toddler. After a couple of miscarriages, Mom was pleased to be pregnant with my brother Timothy. The trouble was that she felt decidedly ill. The family doctor prescribed a new German drug to overcome her feelings of nausea. Despite taking a few tablets the medication had little impact on her sickness, so impetuously she threw the rest of the packet away. It was the best move she ever made. The drug she had dispensed with was thalidomide, which was later linked to physical deformity in babies, including a shortening or complete absence of limbs and malformation of toes and fingers[29].

---

28 A long running BBC television programme aimed at school age children.

29 Fortunately, no children in my primary school suffered from these deformities, but in secondary school there were a few, including one boy in brother Tim's form. Living without fingers but with almost short suckers instead he overcame his difficulties to become top of the form for woodwork.

By the time of my third birthday, Mom was seven months pregnant. There was a modest party in our front room with a few children from round about, specifically Michael and Susan Pheasant, the Pittaway twins and Hayley Skinner from next door but one. I enjoyed the red jelly and homemade birthday cake, blew out the candles and opened my presents. (For the record, I received toys themed around Enid Blyton's Noddy book stories of a Noddy train and Big Ears on a bicycle.)

Far away from jelly and Noddy on a tropical Caribbean Island, communists led by Fidel Castro seized power in Cuba. Soon the new regime was engaging in anti-American rhetoric and cosying up to the Soviets. The development was very bad news for the United States who had an unexpected nuisance on their own back doorstep. Meanwhile, I had not noticed Mom's expanding profile. I knew nothing of Cuba, communism, or conception.

A couple of months later, I distinctly remember being ushered into the back bedroom by Dad to find Mom lying in bed holding a baby. I was told this was my new brother, and his name was Timothy. Mom was smiling and the baby looked peaceful. Being introduced to him for the first time is my earliest memory.

'This is your new brother. What do you think of him?'

Struggling for something meaningful to say, I pointed out that he had bunny rabbits on his pyjamas, which made my parents laugh as he was wrapped in a blanket that had a rabbit design. I had been an only child for just over three years, now that had changed. Tim was elsewhere just now, but soon I would be sharing my bedroom with him, *Noddy* paper and all.

For the first twelve months or so of his life, Tim only seemed to do two things: sleep and cry. His crying was not just grizzling but top of the voice, relentlessly, hour after hour noise. Often, he would send himself to sleep sobbing. Although I did not understand these things, Mom must have been at the end of her tether. I remember her rocking his pram endlessly on the slabs at the back of the house in the hope that the crying would end and the sleep would begin. Despite visits to the GP, she never got to the bottom of the cause of the crying. Now an internet search engine might suggest some intolerance was the cause, maybe milk. Then things were different. As time wore on, the crying would cease and Tim would become more interesting, a good roommate and a best friend to play football with.

By 1961, I had come to terms with the responsibility of being an elder brother and had started school. Significant things were also happening elsewhere. The United States had a new, youthful president in John F. Kennedy. He was eager to make his mark to gain respect at home and to let the Soviets know he was no 'pushover', or 'patsy' as the Americans term it. The 'problem' of Cuba was in his in-tray, and this became an imperative to him. Kennedy turned to the country's Central Intelligence Agency (CIA) for advice and soon decided he needed to topple Castro's regime to create stability amongst his country's near neighbours. (To give some sense of scale, a journey from the Yew Tree Estate to London is thirty miles greater than Cuba is from US shores.) A plan was hatched whereby the CIA would train and arm Cuban exiles and provide landing craft so that an unexpected amphibious assault on the island could take place. Once landed, the exiles would rally support amongst fellow Cubans who would rise to overthrow the new communist regime. It had all the daring of a plot in a *James Bond* movie. Unfortunately, it also had all the credibility of a *James Bond* storyline. By the time 1,200 lightly armed exiles waded ashore at the Bay of Pigs, Cuban aircraft had already sunk their supply ships. Worse still, it became apparent that there was not an appetite for a local uprising. One hundred of the US-backed invaders were killed, and the remainder captured.

The plan was rash, badly conceived and poorly executed; in short, it was a disaster. The invasion will surely figure prominently alongside the Charge of the Light Brigade[30] a century earlier when the definitive volume of all time military blunders is written. There may be something in the British psyche that appreciates and even celebrates heroic failure as it did with the Light Brigade. Lord Cardigan, the blundering leader, was a Battle of Balaclava survivor who went on to become something of a national hero. Such a sentiment is not shared by the American public. Kennedy was far from achieving hero status, and his intervention had made an unfavourable situation far worse.

Soviet military aid to the Cubans followed, which by October 1962 included nuclear missiles pointing northwards towards American cities. US and the Soviet leaders engaged in a tense political and military standoff that lasted for two long weeks. The whole of the world held its breath following developments with trepidation. This was probably as close as the world has ever come to a nuclear conflict that would lead to mutual destruction and complete annihilation of the planet. This was the subject of the overheard conversation at the end of our street.

An uneasy peace was brokered when Kennedy agreed to Soviet leader Nikita Khrushchev's offer to remove the Cuban missiles in exchange for a promise never to invade Cuba. The humiliated US president was also forced into agreeing to remove missiles from Turkey, a fact kept secret at the time. The planet would remain intact, and Yew Tree Estate would survive – for the time being at least.

Castro was celebrated in Latin America and elsewhere as the guy 'who stuck it to Uncle Sam'. Even Che Guevara, who fought alongside him, achieved worldwide cult status as a type of political/pop icon. A frustrated and humiliated US leadership

---

30 The cavalry charge against well-defended Russian artillery during the Crimean war led to carnage and a 40 % casualty rate. The incident was patriotically reported by a sympathetic British press and celebrated in the famous poem by Alfred, Lord Tennyson. Bizarrely the event was generally viewed as heroic rather than foolhardy.

placed a complete trade embargo on its upstart neighbour. The purpose behind the action was spelt out with cold, callous, and cruel honesty *'(to) bring about hunger, desperation, and overthrow of the government.'* Cuba was forced to carve out a new way of life and attempted to become agriculturally self-sufficient. The Soviets supplied animal feed, insecticides, and fertilisers in exchange for sugar. Cigar sales found new markets and new trading partners emerged. An absence of tourists from American was accepted as a necessary casualty of the political situation.

Kennedy saw the issue he inherited as a communist threat too close to home, an unwelcome red chink in the Western bloc. To him it was like a tiny snag in a favourite jumper. Had it not been for the culture he inherited, he might have regarded Cuba as a blemish that did not need to be attended to, an itch that did not need to be scratched.

Culture has a powerful controlling influence that demands acceptance of certain givens and norms and breeds group think. The society I knew had a shared view of the world, and things were very clear. We now lived our lives under the shadow of potential nuclear destruction, and someone was responsible. The Soviets were the villains, while the Americans took on the role of goodies, despite the Cuban missile crisis. When nuclear weapons belong to 'your' side, they represent an independent nuclear deterrent. When they belong to the 'other' side, they are weapons of mass destruction held by unstable regimes.

Goodies and baddies were everywhere, and it was easy to distinguish one from another. Everything and everyone around you conspired to reinforce the same message. There is a battle between good and evil and ultimately good triumphs. This was the formula for most Walt Disney films. The good guys sometimes took the form of honest law enforcement characters, such as TV police officer *Dixon of Dock Green*, who always overcame the criminals. Popular Wild West stories following the *Roy Rogers / The Lone Ranger / Rawhide / Bonanza* tradition told tales of brave cowboys (always wearing light-coloured cowboy hats) fighting off and then succeeding against warring Indians and the bad guys (who helpfully wore black hats). For the most part these were entertaining distractions from the omnipresent threat posed by the Soviets. The issue was obvious and ingrained. The real enemy threatened world peace and society as we knew it. They had a nuclear arsenal and an evil ideology that disrespected individual rights and suppressed religious beliefs. They were unlike us, and we did not really understand them.[31]

If I had looked for evidence of how seriously my parents were taking an impending Armageddon, it was easy to find. Mom had assembled a huge food stock of tinned food in the pantry. This would be enough to withstand a medieval siege, let alone a nuclear bomb – so long as someone had the foresight to put a tin opener with the haul.

Adult conversations sometimes referenced the threat of an imminent nuclear attack, and government advice was given on what to do if the worst came to the worst[32]. This included sheltering under the stairs with a stock of tinned food. There would not be much room under our staircase, but Mom had the food sorted. The threat seemed very real because Western society shared the picture of a vast dust mushroom rising over a devastated Japanese landscape. It was an image imprinted upon our collective consciousnesses. I never stopped to wonder whether ordinary Russians going about their day-to-day business of labouring on farms or working in factories shared the same fear and had seen the same dreadful image we all had.

Fear was a constant undercurrent of ordinary life. Fear of what 'they' might do. From the back garden I could scan the sky for a mushroom cloud of rising dust. If the Soviets had targeted the sewerage plant (of all places), the cloud rising in the sky

---

31 Churchill once described the Soviets as a 'mystery wrapped in an enigma'.

32 Even as late as 1980 the government were funding a public information campaign called Protect and Survive offering advice on what to do in the case of a nuclear attack.

would, in all probability, have not been grey or dusty but brown and smelly. If I had been able to break out of the cultural strait jacket I was born into, I might have been reassured by asking myself what was in it for the Soviets to attack the West? Immediate retaliation would lead to their own destruction. Thankfully, the bombing raids of 6 and 9 August 1945[33], which brought Japanese surrender at the end of a world war, represent the first and last use of nuclear weapons in armed conflict. The Cuban missile crisis seventeen years on from these events was as close as the world ever came to seeing nuclear bombs being used in a similar way.

You tend to make sense of things wearing the cultural lenses you are given. Only as you get older do you question how good those lenses really are and the degree of bias they may have. Sometimes the lenses irritate you and you want none of them. Sometimes you put on different lenses and see events very differently. For those who felt the whole situation was lunacy, there were 'ban the bomb' demonstrations throughout the fifties. The Campaign for Nuclear Disarmament (CND) was founded in 1958 after Britain's own nuclear programme culminated in a nuclear test in Australia and the Pacific. The first meeting of CND in 1958 drew 5,000 people. Calling for unilateral disarmament, several public marches between London and the Aldermaston atomic weapons factory were organised to draw attention to their cause.

Holding nuclear weapons can, in itself, be a dangerous thing. Rich Hall's BBC documentary in 2020 was less of an analysis of the Cold War than a study of human ineptitude and attempted self-harming. The Soviets built a plutonium facility in the Urals,

---

33 Attempting to bring an end to the Second World War as soon as possible, US President Harry Truman had made the fateful decision to detonate two nuclear weapons over the Japanese cities of Hiroshima and Nagasaki. With the blessing of allies and the consent of the United Kingdom the two strikes killed approximately 200,000 civilians. Many not killed outright died later of painful radiation poisoning.

pumping its waste into a river. In 1957, the waste tanks exploded, sending up radioactive clouds to over 270,000 Russian citizens. A mere 11,000 were evacuated, and because of a lack of information being readily available, it is estimated that several hundred may have died. The actual total could be far higher. Not to be outdone, the US Air Force accidentally dropped not one but two nuclear bombs on North Carolina in 1961. One bomb got stuck in a tree and the other came to rest peacefully in a field. Thankfully, neither bomb exploded. Each bomb was 3.8 megatons, 250 times more powerful than the bomb that destroyed Hiroshima. Strangely these events received little newspaper coverage and attention at the time. It is difficult to argue with Hall's conclusion that the Americans were less likely to kill their enemy with nuclear weapons than kill themselves, and the same applied to the Soviets.

Aside from the fear of nuclear weapons, a second type of fear was that there might be traitors in our midst. The possibility of some undercover agent reporting back to Moscow called for constant vigilance. For someone like me, this was completely unnecessary as any traitors who were unmasked were of a different social class altogether and likey to be Cambridge[34] rather than Yew Tree Junior School educated. If the British public were mindful of the issue, then the Americans were paranoid. Fear spawned 'McCarthyism', a fifties version of sustained witch hunts. Led by the then US Senator Joseph McCarthy, the aim was to purge the government of suspected communist infiltration. An unlikely phrase of 'anti-American activities' was coined, and thousands of communists or suspected communists were hauled before public hearings. Those subjected to these trials often faced unsubstantiated allegations which defamed their

---

34 When the Cold War ended, KGB and CIA files confirmed the existence of a spy ring involving Kim Philby, Guy Burgess, Donald Maclean, and Anthony Blunt, all of whom had betrayed their country to spy for the Soviets.

character and reputation. The experience may not have flushed out many traitors, but it did destroy careers and lives.

My birth coincided with a period of national turmoil that became known as 'the Suez Crisis'. The outcome resulted in national humiliation, the cementing of a reputation for a local hero and a narrative of how the imperial bully boys had been defeated. Soon after the birth of my brother, history echoed a similar pattern. This time it involved a period of world crisis and culminated in the humiliation of the United States by a nearby communist leader. The end of the crisis did not end the threat. We all shared a common enemy and 'knew' we were being spied upon. Above all else, we 'knew' that a nuclear button could be pressed at any time with devastating effect. We lived a life under the shadow of the 'bomb'.

# Chapter Six

## *The year of hot and cold*

As 1963 dawned, there was a distinct chill in the air, and it was nothing to do with the weather. Having served as brothers in arms when defeating the Nazi threat, Russia and America had diametrically opposed views on how the world should be politically reconstructed now the war was over. The frosty tension between the two sides threatened to spill over into war at any moment.

The term 'Cold War' was first coined by the English novelist and thinker George Orwell. In a magazine article he described a nuclear stalemate between 'monstrous' super-states, each possessing weapons capable of destroying millions in seconds. By 1963, politicians and the media were using the term extensively as a shorthand for the ongoing battle. In one corner there was Soviet Russia and apparently bleak countries like Czechoslovakia, Hungary, and Poland in support. In the other corner was the United States and the West. Caught between the two was the vanquished Germany, divided to form two new countries, democratic West Germany, and communist East Germany.

The Soviet Union's[35] lived version of the communist philosophy involved a one-party state and control from Moscow. The Union extended over a vast land surface to include fourteen countries adjoining Russia, stretching from the Baltic states of Eastern Europe through north and central Asia to the Pacific Ocean and including over 200 million people living in eleven different time zones. Allied to this there were Eastern European countries like Hungary, led by communist leaders appointed or approved by the Russian leadership. These satellite states ran their countries in synergy with the Soviet Union.

---

35 Also referred to as USSR, The Union of Soviet Socialist Republics.

For someone growing up at the time, this was scary stuff, even if I did not understand all the intricacies. All I 'knew' was that there was an enemy called Russia who was trigger-happy and could wipe me and everyone else from the face of the planet at any point. I never stopped to consider how realistic it was to expect Russia to act like an irrational kamikaze honeybee, knowing full well that it would also be signing its own death warrant.

The Cold War and its implications formed a constant undercurrent to daily life in the Britain of the fifties and sixties. The whole lexicon of the time was loaded. There was the 'free world' (us), and there were those behind the 'iron curtain'[36] (them). During the Second World War, Russia's leader Stalin was nicknamed 'Uncle Joe' by the media for propaganda purposes. Now, the full extent of the ruthlessness of Stalin's leadership was highlighted. He was no longer our friendly relative; he was public enemy number one. Having overseen the development of nuclear weapons as well as purges against various groups and starvation among peasants, Stalin was succeeded by Khrushchev in 1953. The Soviet influence showed no sign of abating under its new leader.

One Cold War standoff was centred on Vietnam. With the Viet Cong wishing to unify the country under a Soviet-style regime, opponents in the south of the country were supported by America. What ensued was an ongoing conflict that began in 1954[37] and continued for over twenty long years. Three million died, and direct American involvement drew opposition at home and amongst her closest allies. The British government managed to keep the country out of direct conflict but stopped

---

36  In 1946 former Prime Minister Winston Churchill stressed the menace of Soviet communism, which had lowered an 'iron curtain' over Europe.

37  Similarly, in a conflict between North and South Korea between 1950 and 1953 the North were backed by the Soviets and China, and the South by USA and its allies.

short of criticising the Americans, with good reason, we owed them a fortune in debt payments run up during the war.

One high-profile American dissenter was world champion boxer and activist Muhammed Ali. Regarded by many as the greatest boxer of all time, Ali was also a campaigning figure. In 1964 he changed his birth name from Cassius Clay as it was a 'slave name'. He converted to the Islam faith and was a significant figurehead for African Americans and the civil rights movement. At the height of the war, he refused to be drafted as he had 'no quarrel with the Vietcong'. He may have been stripped of his boxing titles, banned from boxing in the US[38], and criminally convicted of refusal to be inducted into the US Army, but Ali remained unrepentant.

Apart from engaging in the wars of others, other proxies were found to evidence superiority with no direct physical battle going on. Both sides seized on anything and everything as a propaganda tool to reinforce their own position. Sport proved a good battlefield. Here, the US could take on the USSR in basketball, ice hockey and, as unlikely as it seems, chess. The propaganda value of victory was immense. Even literature became a tool in the Cold War. America's Central Intelligence Agency (CIA) financed the printing of a Russian edition of Boris Pasternak's book *Doctor Zhivago* for distribution to any Russian straying this side of the Iron Curtain. (The book was banned in the USSR.) When Pasternak won the Nobel Prize for Literature, there were suspicions that the CIA had leaned on the committee responsible for recommending the award.

The intrigue, espionage and subversionary tactics employed in the Cold War were all captured as a theme and then glamorised by the fictional but hugely popular *James Bond* films of the period. Sean Connery did not so much play James Bond as be

---

38 Ali was banned from the ring for nearly three years but regained his title in 1974.

James Bond, a secret agent with a licence to kill. (It was OK; he was only going to kill baddies who wished us harm. The bonus was that he would do this with charm and humour). Mom and Dad, like millions of Westerners, loved these films.

If sport, literature, films, and press coverage were grist for the mill, more spectacularly still, the war found expression in space exploration. Technological advancements meant an escalating capability of both sides to blow everyone off the face of the planet. Technological superiority could be most visible, however, in the space programmes of the era. Inevitably described as the 'space race', the finishing line was defined in 1961 by US President John F. Kennedy as 'landing a man (sic) on the moon'. This represented a very public challenge to both sides. Commenting that 'we choose to go to the moon because it is difficult, not easy', he set the end of the decade as a target. The desire to reach the target (and considerable resources thrown at the scheme) forced technological advances previously unimaginable.

A quiet corner of Cheshire may seem far removed from the Cold War, or indeed anything remarkable. Nothing could be farther from the truth. There is an unlikely connection between the area and India's Taj Mahal, the Great Barrier Reef, and the pyramids of Giza. The Jodrell Bank Observatory, Cheshire, shares the distinction of joining these iconic and culturally important sites as a UNESCO World Heritage site. The Observatory pioneered the science of radio astronomy by using radio waves instead of visible light when researching the universe. The huge Lovell Telescope was able to track US and Russian craft during the space race. The highlight was not only tracking the first spacecraft to make a soft landing on the moon, but also the coup of being able to print the first picture from the lunar surface. By 1963, Jodrell Bank was also being used as the UK's early warning system against any potential nuclear attack.

If the newspapers were full of the Cuban Missile Crisis the year previous, then there was a more salacious dimension to the news coverage of 1963. An unusual subplot to the Cold War involved a hot affair that provided steamy copy for the newspapers and nearly brought down the government there and then. In March, John Profumo, the Secretary of State for War, lied to parliament when denying an affair with Christine Keeler, a nineteen-year-old would-be model. The issue was less about morality and more about security. It also raised issues of public trust in the establishment. When the press reported the Profumo–Keeler affair, the additional twist to the tale was that Keeler may have been simultaneously involved with a supposed Soviet naval attaché, Captain Yevgeny Ivanov, most likely a spy. The newspapers unrelentingly played out the potential for shared pillow talk and compromised security. The affair ended Profumo's political career and gave Keeler an opportunity to obtain celebrity status[39].

It is worth reflecting on John Profumo's title in the government of the day. A Minister for War is a strange office to hold in peacetime. These were however no ordinary times, and the country was part of the ongoing Cold War. The country had known the carnage of two world wars, and there was a real fear of an even more terrible war just around the corner. Decades on, and in less paranoid times, a modern equivalent for the post might be Defence Secretary. It might be naive and unduly optimistic, but it would mark a real achievement of a civilised world if a future cabinet post was designated Minister for Peace.

There is a childhood game that involves hiding an object, and when your play mate searches for it, giving clues by simply saying either 'hot' or 'cold.' One spring day I devised my own version of the game. Our house had a basic verandah at the back of the house involving a couple of feet of brickwork topped with panes of glass like an oversized greenhouse. The verandah housed things that failed to make it into the house, like shoes and boxes, as well as having cupboards packed with potentially useful

---

39 The black and white portrait of a naked Christine Keeler staring back at the camera while straddling the back of a chair remains one of the iconic images of the era. The photograph taken by late Australian photographer Lewis Morley.

stuff. I noticed that there was a small gap between the verandah and the fence, so I decided to hide there and watch my family look for me. I observed them getting more desperate by the minute as they searched for me, walking up and down the garden and looking in the garage and shed. It was a terrible thing to do. Eventually, Mom found me and, instead of telling me off, tutted good humouredly and said she thought that was where I would be. The obvious question was, of course, as to why I did it. Unfortunately, it was a question I could not answer.

Nationally, the ongoing Cold War and a hot affair gave way to white heat in September. Scarborough can be a pleasantly warm Yorkshire seaside resort but is not really associated with intense heat. Yet this was the setting for the leader of the opposition, Harold Wilson, to deliver one of the most memorable political speeches of the century[40]. Reflecting on the pace of technological change and its implications for industry, Wilson warned that for the country to prosper, a 'new Britain' would need to be forged in the 'white heat' of this 'scientific revolution'. One observer commented that Wilson had succeeded in 'capturing science' for the Labour Party. With the government rocking from the Profumo Affair, they had also surrendered the technological initiative to the opposition. The next year's general election saw the Conservative Party voted from office.

By winter, the country was still in the grip of the worst conditions within living memory. Plummeting temperatures caused rivers, lakes, and even the sea to freeze over. The country experienced its first white Christmas in years with snowdrifts, some of which were twenty feet high. Travel by roads and rail was impossible, snow brought down electricity cables and telephone lines, and remote communities were isolated for days on end. Many animals died of starvation in the snow, with farmers unable to reach them. The 'Big Freeze' of 1963 was officially one of the coldest winters on record.

---

40 See Chapter twelve also.

Football is a game traditionally played in all weathers, but there were four hundred matches postponed over the winter period, the biggest disruption since the outbreak of war in 1939. Betting on games and the operation of the pools was big business. Apart from individuals like Grandad, who had their wagers collected by agents on a Friday evening, virtually every workplace had a pools syndicate whereby a whole department or office engaged in a corporate 'flutter'. As a response to the freeze, a pools panel was created made up of experts and given the job of producing hypothetical results so that the football pools could continue operating[41]. The cross of the biro on a square on the pools coupon (indicating a draw) has now been replaced by the cross of the fingers on the National Lottery symbol. The National Lottery was not introduced until 1994, and up until that point the pools companies ruled supreme.

On the estate, snow was cleared from the road and piled on the edge of pavements and grass verges to make the estate navigable by car. Even then the surface of the road resembled glass. Meanwhile, the crunchy snow-packed pavements were treacherously exciting.

By the time I celebrated my eighth birthday in late January, the weather was still bad. Snowmen built in back gardens looked sad and shabby by the time Yew Tree Junior and Infant school was reopened. Somehow, Mom managed the school run with a pre-school Timothy in tow. When the school milk was delivered around mid-morning, it was rock solid with the glass of the bottle taking on a frosty mist. It was at this point that the value of the milk monitors became apparent. They went around the school placing as many bottles as possible into the crevices on the huge

---

41 In a pre-National Lottery age 'the pools' involving predicting the outcome of matches and was the nation's most popular low-cost betting flutter. Each match had a number allocated to it, but Grandad preferred to stick to the same numbers in the hope of predicting ten games that would be score draws, so winning him the jackpot.

metal radiators. By lunchtime, the milk was one-third ice lolly and two-thirds thawed, taking on a slight yogurt-like flavour.

Ten minutes before the close of the school day, the light outside was fading fast, and the class was told to prepare themselves for the home time exit. We were wilting in our coats and wellingtons, waiting for the exact time to arrive before making it outside. Most of us had, at this point, also put our heads through knitted balaclavas. The journey home would be an opportunity to ride imaginary horses through the snow like chain-mailed riders we had seen dozens of times before on the television programme *The Adventures of Robin Hood*[42]. I was surely not alone in mentally singing the programme's theme tune as I pulled on my balaclava, 'Robin Hood, Robin Hood riding through the glen, Robin Hood with his band of men, da, da, da, ... loved by the poor ... da, da, da, Robin Hood, Robin Hood ...'

The year may have been politically significant in Britain, but globally it was just another year of engagement in the Cold War. 1963 was a time of hot and cold.

---

42 The thirty-minute black and white television programme starring Richard Greene was first broadcast on the commercial channel ATV in 1955.

# EVERYDAY LIFE

# Chapter Seven

## *School days*

A single, certain day shortly after my fifth birthday was a day like no other. There was no fuss or pre-warning. I did all the normal things. I got up, washed, put on my everyday clothes, and had breakfast. There were no clues as to what lay in store for me. Soon however I found myself in my warm coat, marching alongside Mom. Tim was grizzling as Mom purposefully propelled him in his pushchair towards the other side of the estate. We were not alone, it seemed that half the kids I knew, and some I did not, were all heading in the same direction, making sounds like a noisy flock of migrating birds.

I simply walked to my first day at school. There had been no preparation, no induction, no pre-school, no nursery; I cannot even remember it being discussed beforehand, although it must have been. Finding myself in an alien place with neither of my parents in attendance could have been distressing, but there were plenty of children I knew, and the place looked inviting and potentially exciting. I never gave a thought as to whether Mom could cope with Tim without me, I was far too distracted by other matters. Important matters. My attention instead was on keeping letters and numbers within the lines of the 'rough' book I had been issued with. Then there was sitting on the story mat without wriggling and getting the attention of Miss by raising my arm rigidly in the air and grunting slightly. Here I was, a child grown up enough to go to school for the first time, an event that was not in any way traumatic, just very different.

Yew Tree Infant and Juniors was a normal state school, modern for its time and built as part of the estate's development. Although the facilities were spartan and unsophisticated by today's standards, I never wanted for anything. Books, writing and art materials, as well as display boards and chalkboards, were all in good supply. Teachers and the Headteacher were unencumbered by ratios, key performance indicators, budgets, and savings targets. Instead, they concerned  themselves with teaching, some very well.

The school was ambitious and, while I was there, a small swimming pool was built on the site. What is remarkable is that the cost of the pool was financed by raising the necessary funds locally. Pupils brought a set contribution of a silver coin or two every week in return for being members of the 'dolphin club' and getting a sticker. The Parent Teachers Association (PTA) went into overdrive. Every fundraising event included an appeal for the purchase of a brick for just 'half a crown'[43]. Parents volunteered to help with digging out the foundations, bricklaying, and painting. When the pool was completed, we had an additional lesson on the timetable. Mrs Spears had her own approach to teaching swimming by wearing Wellington boots and a transparent pac-a-mac (a fold-away raincoat that was very popular at the time). She would pace around the pool, shouting instructions and encouragement. Goodness knows what would have happened if any of us had got into difficulty and needed rescuing. After a half hour session, we would emerge from the pool with chloride-induced streaming eyes and stiffened hair. After a couple of years of splashing and thrashing about every week everyone learned how to stay afloat and swim, including me.

There were of course sacrifices involved in going to school. Things like missing *Watch with Mother* on afternoon television. I was now a school child. I had apparently outgrown *Andy Pandy* and his playmates Looby Loo and Teddy. Bill and Ben, *The Flower Pot Men* with their strange speech and stranger relationship with a little weed, would have to continue without me, as would *The Woodentops* with their bizarre movement and

---

43 Now twelve and half pence.

unconvincing puppet strings[44]. There were however compensations to being at school, including my very own bottle of milk. In common with every other school child, there was a small bottle of milk to look forward to every morning. The milk was guzzled through a stubby, increasingly soggy straw at morning break (designated 'playtime'). Good nutrition had been identified as key to effective learning by a forward-thinking government, and milk was also argued to be an anti-poverty measure that would help combat malnutrition[45]. The 1945 Free School Milk Act gave every school child under the age of eighteen the right to a third of a pint of milk each school day[46].

Having milk in your class meant that you needed monitors. Those vested with the honour of being a milk monitor had the privilege of lumping bottles about. Full crates of bottles were moved into the classroom on a small trolley and, once consumed, returned to the entrance hall for the caretaker to deal with. Being a milk monitor was a highly prestigious role with its use of specialist equipment (a trolley) and a uniform that came with the job. 'Uniforms' were rough cotton aprons a helpful member of the PTA had doubtless run up on a *Singer* sewing machine.

Becoming a monitor was a badge of honour bestowed entirely at the class teacher's whim, and there were monitors appointed for

---

44 The TV programme started before I was born (in 1953) and ran for twenty years. The only programme with a target audience of preschool children, it had its genesis in the radio show Listen with Mother. The BBC tagged both programmes with the words 'with mother' to counter fears it was encouraging bad parenting by adults who might just dump their children in front of TV or radio sets to engage with the programmes alone.

45 The scheme also extended to pregnant women.

46 The practice lasted until the then Education Secretary Margaret 'Thatcher the snatcher' intervened in the early seventies.

a variety of roles. Monitors were seduced into thinking they were special when in practice they were dogsbodies entrusted with low-level tasks. Plant monitors had to water the busy lizzie pot plants that shared the low windowsills with dead flies. Windows monitors were required to open the windows in the classroom. The job was not always straightforward as some windows had been heavily gloss painted, which formed a tight seal that was hard to budge. Higher windows could only be opened by using a pole that ended spectacularly with a brass hook, which fitted a circle incorporated into the steel frame. Being a plant or windows monitor was OK, but the plumb job was register monitor. Robert Shelley was always chosen for the role. This involved him taking time out to wander along the corridors to the school secretary's office with the day's dinner money and attendance register.

Robert enjoyed access to a place which was normally off limits. The office functioned as a barrier to the Head's room. When the door was open it was possible to see interesting things like swivel chairs, charts, a phone, and a chunky black typewriter. The room itself was dominated by a huge *Gestetner* duplicating machine that came complete with a large handle and the smell of ink. Sometimes one brand becomes so familiar that it becomes a verb. Nowadays, expressions like 'I will just Google that' are used as a shorthand for using an online search engine, just as 'hoovering up' signifies vacuuming the floor. Conversations between teachers referenced getting letters 'gestetnered' in advance of home time. My memory of school days is strongest when being reminded of the comforting smells of the place, including the distinctive aroma of the fuzzy blue ink on the gestetner produced letters that we took home to our parents. Then there was the smell of the hall at lunchtime, and the evocative wet cut grass smell of the school field, which was most obvious when the windows monitors had done their job correctly. The most potent aroma of all however was the antiseptic notes of the floor cleaner, which could catch you off guard and attack your nasal passages if you were not careful.

My experience of school was at odds with the books that were read to me by the teacher at story time and Mom at home. These stories had school age heroes with names like William or Jennings. It was very confusing; why, for instance, did I go home at the end of the school day? Why didn't I stay with school chums to have adventures and then sleep in the dormitory? Why didn't I have classmates with names like Cartwright Minor or Julian or Arabella? Why didn't we use phrases like 'wizard', 'gosh', or 'jolly good' or get up to adventures after dark or engage in detective investigations? What was wrong with Yew Tree Infant and Junior School? Rather than making time for such goings on, the school day was built around routines like: hang coats up, story time, register, writing, milk, sums, lunch, art and craft, playtime, reading, coats on, and home time.

The daily ritual also included a morning school assembly where classes of children filed into the school gymnasium/school hall to sit down on the parquet flooring in neat rows. What normally followed involved fidgeting through housekeeping notices and then engaging in a sort of mini-church service. Today, projected computer *PowerPoint* presentations make the use of acetate slides and overhead projectors (OHP) seem dated. An OHP would have proved revolutionary if the school had just possessed one. Instead, there were two giant hymn books suspended on strategically placed pulleys connected to the rafters of the hall. On cue, assembly monitors would lower the sheets, search for the correct hymn, and then raise the words just high enough to see. Often, the two chosen hymns would be sandwiched by the telling of a story from the bible. Sometimes the event would end with a speedy recital of the Lord's prayer, with not everyone getting every word right ('… witches art in heaven …').

The bible stories were easy to understand but offered no context. This once led me to think that both the newborn Moses and baby Jesus escaped the same terror of infant slaying even though the stories occurred at different ends of the bible and were separated by a gap of 1,600 years. I have more recently attended my grandsons' school assemblies, which are vastly different by nature. These sometimes highlight a religious festival from a major world faith but are light on content. Instead, the assemblies seem to aim to celebrate pupil attainment and stress themes of general morality, which is good. The problem however is that unchurched children are growing up unaware of stories, some shared by three major world faiths. The significance of things encountered in everyday life is lost as a result. For instance, youngsters may hear but not understand why sports commentators reference David versus Goliath when a favourite of superior ability plays against an underdog. Then there are journalists, politicians and advertisers employing terms like 'being a good Samaritan', 'prodigals returning', 'Damascus Road type conversion' or using expressions like 'manna from heaven' and 'turning the other cheek'. The fading knowledge of basic bible stories is creating a cultural deficit.

A 'where were you when ...' moment is often applied to momentous events. One such event, for those old enough to remember, was the Dallas assassination of John Fitzgerald Kennedy, the thirty-fifth President of the United States. While I do not remember first hearing the news, I vividly remember a minute's silence being impeccably observed in the school assembly. The solemnity of the occasion had been heightened by a stirring address by Mr Tolley, the Headteacher, who told us that JFK had been a great man. Most fixed their eyes downwards while others fought back their tears. I stared at a huge clock on the front wall and contemplated a modern-day saint brutally cut down in his prime.

Nobody deserves to have their life taken from them, and certainly not in the way Kennedy had. Maybe a great man had died that day in November 1963, however I suppose it depends on how you define greatness. It seems to me now that Kennedy had major faults and was not really saint material. Not that this necessarily makes him a bad person, just a poor choice as a saint. What is true is that he brought the world to the brink of nuclear destruction by his mishandling of the Cuban missile crisis. He also invested billions of dollars in the space race when a more

worthy use of money and political effort might have been directed towards fighting rampant racial discrimination in his own
country. A contemporary of Kennedy was the civil rights leader Martin Luther King Jr., who was also assassinated. Surely,
he was a more worthy candidate to be considered great in the
saint/martyr mould?

The radio (or 'wireless' as older teachers insisted on calling
it) was used to provide twice-weekly music lessons. This relied
on impeccable timing on behalf of the teacher to get the class
settled and then tune in just at the right time using a knob the
size of a roll of *Sellotape* in the process. Lessons involved the
lusty singing of folk and other songs over and over. The lyrics
told vivid stories of a soldier delaying marriage because he did
not have a coat to put on, huge Derbyshire Rams, the surviv-
al instincts of the victor of Bray and sea shanties about sailors
drinking rum. Then there were minstrel songs like the *Camptown
Ladies* and Scottish tales of Bonny Prince Charlie. It must have
been fascinating to hear young contorted Black Country voices
mimicking the many different dialects.

On an allotted morning, it was the turn of my class to use the
hall for Physical Education (PE), and sometimes the radio was
again used as an aid. A plummy female voice prompted us to join
in with 'music, movement and mime' for twenty minutes or so.
Just pretending that loose sand was running through your fingers did not seem much like physical exercise, but PE lessons
were strange affairs, particularly when we were still in the infant
classes. The changing arrangements involved the boys decant-
ing into a storeroom, where we took off our shirts to reveal our
white vests and put on our elasticated pumps. The girls 'changed'
in the classroom. This involved them tucking their skirts into
their knickers and putting on different footwear. We then met
up again in the hall, where we all ran around, attempted to use
hula-hoops, eyed beanbags curiously, and undertook supposedly healthy exercises which the teacher devised apparently off
the top of her head.

By the time I reached junior school age, I realised that schoolgirls were different from boys and not just physically. It manifested itself in the things that girls did at playtimes. Some had corking sets they busied themselves with. Corking involved wrapping multi-coloured wool around four nails on the end of an empty wooden cotton reel to produce a strip of something that looked like knitting. Exactly what they did with the finished product I am not sure. Girls possessed an innate ability to play recorders and use skipping ropes properly. These things I imagined were exceedingly difficult to do with any sort of proficiency if you were a boy. They also had whispered chats about 'girl things'. We boys hung about talking or played tag.

Chats in the playground often led to us boys engaging in a wild goose chase for something or other. For instance, one lad once said that if you had a bun penny, it was worth a lot of money. (Some older coins in circulation still bore the image of Queen Victoria. Earlier in her reign, pennies were minted with the image of a young queen with her hair in a bun.) Every child inspected the loose change in their pocket money and any change their parents had on them at home and reported back day after day. No one had a bun penny. Then someone said that if you managed to collect both a pink and a white clover flower, then it was lucky. Another disagreed and said it was a four-leaved clover. Either way, at lunchtime there was the strange spectacle of groups of boys scrabbling about on their hands and knees on the school field.

There were several strange rules, one of which I once fell foul of. It was a rule that infant school children had to 'play' at one end of the playground and junior school children at the other. For whatever reason I found myself at the wrong end of the playground one day and was stopped in my tracks by the sound of a shrill whistle. Miss Llewelyn, who never seemed to like me very much, asked me what I thought I was doing. As I did not know, I did not answer. After repeating the question a couple of times, she took me by my elbows and shook me. Everyone looked on in shock, and it made me feel a bit sick and very humiliated. I had been on the receiving end of corporal punishment. I never told Mom or Dad because of the shame I felt. This was a pity as both my parents could argue their rights, and Dad would not have minced his words when giving Miss Llewelyn a dressing down. Aside from 'shaking', the other form of punishment was having to stand at the front of the room staring at your classmates sitting at their low tables. I later found out that Secondary School was completely different. Deterrents against misbehaviour and substandard performance were extensively used and included detention and writing lines (repeatedly writing lines like 'I must not run in the corridor'). In terms of corporal punishment, the use of a stick to inflict a rap across the knuckles[47] was administered only by the Head after an appropriate entry in a register. The woodwork teacher ignored these niceties and dealt with the matter himself with the help of a 'remembering' stick.

Apart from Mr Tolley, the headteacher, there was just one male teacher on the staff, Mr Woodward. Inevitably, the poor soul was landed with the job of running the school football team. This involved him sacrificing Saturday mornings and ensuring that everyone had washed the kit in time for the next game. He also missed the normal fish and chips school dinner on a Friday, thanks to a weekly session he ran on the school field. Anyone interested in playing for the team just turned up. A jog around the perimeter of the pitch was followed by Mr Woodward refereeing a brief game of 'probables' versus 'possibles'. Here, undersized footballers played on an oversized pitch with ridiculously tall goalposts and a heavy brown case ball. Mr Woodward would announce the team for the following day at the close of the session.

I made the school team on two occasions. The first match went well for me. I did not see much of the ball or indeed the play, as

---

47 Corporal punishment in state schools was only outlawed as late as 1986.

all the action seemed to take place on the other side of the field. To a passing stranger the match must have resembled something like two packs of dogs chasing a balloon on a windy beach. The following week I was chosen again, presumably on the grounds that although I had not done much, what I had done had not been counterproductive. My second game was different with all the play on my side of the field. There were three bad fouls committed throughout the game, all out of clumsiness rather than malice. All three fouls had been committed by me. I hoped Mr Woodward had not noticed. Our team won 2-0.

I was walking off the field at full time when Mr Woodward caught up with me. He had noticed after all. 'I didn't realise you were such a rough player, Robert.' Those words hit me like a sledgehammer. What I disliked most was being called 'Robert'. It was not an ordinary 'Robert' like the way he said it in class. It was a 'Robert' with an inflection. My name was being used in a critical way. I cannot think Bobby Charlton or Bobby Moore were described as rough by their teacher or accused of being 'Robert'. I was never picked to play for the school team again.

I struggled with rudimentary French, Maths and Science but enjoyed History and English and even excelled at Art. I found out that I had an awful singing voice and could not hold a tune. I was not told in as many words, of course. Instead, I was asked to sing more quietly in assembly and music lessons as it was putting the other children off! On the upside, I also discovered that I had the knack of making my classmates laugh and entertained the whole school on a couple of occasions. There was a tradition of the last afternoon at school before the Christmas break to hold a 'fun' assembly/talent competition. This normally involved girls playing recorders and singing about the holly and ivy or someone reading out a Christmas poem. I made my own contribution by attempting to do an impression of a comedian of the time, Freddy 'Parrotface' Davies. A stand-up comedian, Davies was really a throwback to a music hall entertainer whose act involved telling a story about a parrot. He had a hat pulled down to make his ears stick out and told the stories blowing raspberries as he did so. My act lasted about two minutes and involved retelling one of the jokes that I had heard him deliver on television. Everyone thought it was hilarious, probably because it was so bad an impression that it was good and no one else was setting out to 'do' comedy. The event culminated in a tradition of singing the 'We Wish You a Merry Christmas' song. When the appropriate verse was reached, everyone shouted the words 'We all like  figgy pudding, for we all like figgy pudding, so bring some out here ...' at the top of their very high-pitched voices.

In my last year at junior school, my parents had a big decision to make. It was possible to request that your child take the dreaded 'eleven plus' exam to move on to a secondary school that used academic selection criteria. Such a choice involved risk, as failure would have meant going to a school known as a 'secondary modern' senior school and so carry the stigma of failure through secondary school life and beyond. The default position was not to take the exam and graduate to the large comprehensive school, Churchfields. Although I was far from the brightest in my class, Mom and Dad determined that I would sit the exam. Possibly against the odds, I graduated from Yew Tree Junior school with an eleven plus exam pass. This gave me the right to attend the local grammar school, but Mom and Dad opted that I should go to Technical High, a more technical rather than purely academic secondary school. I was about to find out that the secondary school environment was much more hostile and bruising than anything I had ever experienced before. For now, however, primary school days were, for me, golden days. School days ... happy days.

# Chapter Eight

## *Holidays*

Long school holidays represented an opportunity to play foot-ball for hours on end at the Common at the end of the road. If numbers were lacking rush back goalkeepers ('rushies') would be employed. Sides were picked or just evolved as boys joined in at different stages of the game. Occasionally some disappeared, having been fetched by a younger sibling to 'come in for tea'. These absences might only last twenty minutes or so before they re-emerged to continue playing. The streetlamp helped illumi-nate at least one goal. Indeed it also functioned as a goalpost, so it was possible to play until dusk. Scores could be along the lines of thirty-one goals to twenty-nine, or a more structured approach of 'ten half time, twenty the winner' might be agreed upon. Arguments over scorekeeping would often lead to pre-maturely abandoned games. When on my own, I might kick the ball against the wall on the shared drive between the houses, or two or three would join in for a game of 'slam'. A tumble on this surface normally involved Mom removing gravel from my knee with love, care, and a pair of tweezers sterilised in boiling water. Once clear of gravel, the knee could be plastered in cold pink *Germolene* cream, which had a smell of its own.

When not playing football, Mom might take Tim and my-self for a long walk, or a few of us would hang about together. Our garden was long and narrow with a lawn leading onto a vegetable patch. Sometimes Mom would give us a small bowl of sugar each so we could pick a stick of rhubarb to eat. It was of little consequence that the rhubarb was unwashed. (Matters could have been worse; older gardeners swore by horse manure to promote a healthy growth of the plant.) The bottom of the garden bordered a neglected area of land, which offered a route to classmate Ian Houghton's back garden in Pinewood Close, a cul-de-sac off Lilac Avenue. Avoiding the prolific growth of nettles on the wasteland, we would charge about pretending to be on a secret mission, or similar, and emerge at the foot of Pinewood Close. Where Lilac Avenue met the top of Pinewood Close, the Stallard family lived. Paul Stallard played with us sometimes. His mom was a formidable-looking lady who always wore a black cardigan which had a chain of safety pins attached 'just in case'. She might reach into her cardigan pocket and pull out a packet of red jelly and then break off lumps for us to chew like a toffee. As we got older, a few of us might take off on bikes to Merrion's Wood, crossing the busy Sutton Road along the way. Then there was Barr Beacon, a green hill on the edge of the Walsall conurbation, which offered a vantage point to see for miles, fly a kite or eat an ice cream from the van that always parked there.

School holidays meant a break from the routine of formal education and the start of endless sunny days. Taking a family holiday away from home was a different proposition in terms of weather, and I can only ever remember overcast skies at best.

The Second World War, twenty-odd years earlier, had brought the need for gas masks, food rationing and austerity at home. Despite this, the country's entrepreneurial spirit was far from stifled. Billy Butlin's plans for a holiday camp at Filey on the North Yorkshire coast were put on hold with the outbreak of war in 1939. Undeterred, he persuaded the Ministry of Defence to take on the camp and complete it. When he succeeded, he suggested the construction of two more camps for training purposes, conveniently sited by the coast. Again, he got agreement. When the war ended, Butlin reclaimed the camps and offered working-class families an opportunity to take advantage of the freedom peace offered with an affordable holiday. With hotels out of the price range of most household budgets, the holiday camps were certainly an option. Alternatives included camping, the success of which relied on the vagaries of the weather, cramped caravan holidays or the prospect of having to deal with the legendary landladies who ran bed and breakfast (B and B) seaside outfits with fierce efficiency.

*Butlins* and *Pontins* were the market leaders for holiday camps. Their holidays came complete with some fancy trappings such as entertainment 'blue coats' and fun fairs. There were smaller operators applying the same business model, but without the frills. Mom and Dad opted for one, *Trustville Holiday Camp*, near Mablethorpe on the Lincolnshire coast. The journey to get there seemed never ending with mile after mile in an alien flat landscape with ploughed fields and a faint smell of cabbage. Once there our home for the week was a wooden hut suitably kitted out. Mom continued to cook meals during the holiday from the modest cooker that was in our hut. The site had a social club, shop, post box and communal showers. A programme of activities included a sports day, the bonny baby contest, treasure hunts and, reflecting the culture of the time, the glamorous grandmother competition. We would walk to the social club early evening, where a band played music and Mom and Dad would dance together. The band knew what the floor fillers were. A few numbers would set the children off jumping around in a manic fashion. Their version of *'March of the Mods'*, *'Lilly the Pink'*, and *'Yellow Submarine'* proved hugely popular amongst the kids. We stayed up later than normal and drank fizzy orange juice. We were on holiday.

Outside the camp, the flat sandy beach was bordered by steps to a long concrete promenade. The skies were invariably a forbidding grey, complementing the steel colour of the cold North Sea perfectly. During my childhood, pocket-sized *I-spy books* were popular, making an ideal stocking filler or an affordable pocket money buy. The book consisted of a series of pen and ink drawings for the reader to spot on themes such as 'at the zoo' or 'dogs'. The idea was that you were a Native American with the job of ticking off as many of the items as possible to report back to Big Chief I-Spy. I once took an *I-spy book* 'at the seaside' on holiday with me. I only spotted one type of shell on the beach, namely the razor shell. I suspect that Big Chief I-Spy was disappointed!

I cannot remember taking my jumper off, seeing the sun or being completely warm. Not that this mattered. If we were not on the beach in deck chairs or squatting on sandy blankets eating picnic food, Tim and I were playing 'three goals and in', often using empty wind shelters as goal posts. Another genteel holiday destination, Sutton on Sea, was close by, so all four of us might take a stroll there.

We were there in the summer of 1964, and as we sat on the beach it seemed such a peaceful place. The only other people on the beach were in family groups insulated by wind shields, enjoying their time together. Apart from the whistling wind, the only sounds were the call of the gulls and the roar of the tide. It is difficult to imagine the contrast a few months earlier when, on spring bank holiday weekend, a seaside beach was transformed into a battle scene. The pebbled beach at Brighton became the scene of adolescent rebellion when 2,000 youngsters descended on the place to engage in a violent free-for-all, where even deckchairs were used as weapons. The groups doing the fighting were two rival subcultures, the sharply dressed mods who arrived on multiple mirrored *Vespa* and *Lambretta* motor scooters and the rockers with their black leather jackets and noisy British-made motorbikes like *Triumph, BSA* and *Norton*.

Fifteen miles from the Yew Tree estate in Tamworth, a motor manufacturer had taken the concept of the motorbike and transformed it into something no self-respecting rocker would approve of. Reliant hit on the idea of building lightweight, three-wheeled vehicles made of fibreglass. Their vehicles offered many advantages. The costs were modest, fibreglass meant no rust, and most significantly, some models could be driven by someone holding only a motorcycle licence. For thirty-odd years their vehicles sold in vast numbers. For a while we had one such vehicle in light blue colour.

One year, Mom and Dad decided we would have a holiday in Weston-Super-Mare on the North Somerset coast for a change. Having a *Reliant* meant it was a squash for the four of us and all the things we needed for a week away. Dad had the bright idea of borrowing a roof rack to take an additional suitcase.

Making the 100-plus mile journey, we only got as far as Bristol. When negotiating a corner, the vehicle toppled over completely. The *Reliant* had proved unreliable, or, to be fair, destabilised. I remember everything falling on me and bystanders, including a Teddy boy, rolling the vehicle upright again. Dad went by ambulance to have a broken arm treated, and a kind couple took us into their home to stay for a while and have something to eat. Mr Simms came to rescue us in his older but more spacious and substantial car later in the early evening. We borrowed cases to get everything home. After this, we reverted to plan A for holidays, namely *Trustville Holiday Camp*, near Mablethorpe.

A common feature of many industries of the period was the 'factory fortnight'. Rather than giving workers discretion over when to take their leave, there was an enforced shutdown. While a skeleton staff serviced machinery, workers were free to be with their families during the summer school holidays. Northern workers naturally favoured the nearby Lancastrian coast, and Blackpool became a natural bolt-hole for thousands. Black country workers, by comparison, had more of a decision to make since they lived in the most landlocked area in the country. Some opted to make the journey to the seaside towns in the Northwest, others to the Welsh coast. We had day trips and short caravan holidays, sometimes with Nan and Grandad, to destinations such as Rhyl on the Welsh coast. Nan and Grandad liked Blackpool and had several holidays there, taking advantage of one of the pastel-coloured boarding houses, which were fragrant with morning after morning of breakfast fry-ups. They returned from their holiday with virtually the same photograph every year – a snap of them taken on the promenade. They did not own a camera themselves, but a photographer would take a picture, give them a ticket, and a couple of hours later they could collect the memento for an appropriate fee. The picture would go on the shelf over the fire along with Royal British Legion poppies that they reused every November. The snapshot would doubtless jolt memories for them of a change of scenery, visiting Blackpool tower, and a nice cup of tea in 'Andy's Café'.

Blackpool was the epitome of a British working-class holiday resort. It had all the key trappings of amusement arcades, a pier, deckchairs, and donkey rides. It was quite unlike Mablethorpe. Unashamedly 'tacky', shops packed with tasteless souvenirs were as prolific as notices to stay away from the sea because of the dangers of raw sewage. On the plus side there was the attraction of illuminated trams, chips in newspaper wrappings and the chance to be sandblasted walking along the sea front. The whole place seemed to be orientated towards machines designed to entice you to part with your pocket money. Apart from the amusement arcades with their claw machines, penny falls, and pinball machines, there were coin-operated machines everywhere. There were pay-to-view telescopes trained on the horizon, while other machines dispensed measured quantities of nuts or sweets for a fee. Teenagers crammed into photo booths in 'kiss me quick' hats for a strip of candid snapshots. For grown ups , machines dispensed a card with your weight or your fortune on it. The most disturbing coin-operated machine of all involved a huge glass box that housed a life-sized ventriloquist's dummy seated on a throne, wearing a crown, and holding a doll in a jester's outfit. The appropriate coin would jolt the dummy to life so that he rocked backward and forward to a sound of inane laughter. The whole experience was unnerving rather than amusing with the opaque eyes, the machine-like rocking, and the pathetic laughter. When the experience ended, the dummy would fix you with his lifeless eyes, inviting you to dispense another coin. I never did. Was this machine a metaphor for a certain holiday experience, unsatisfying, unreal, and a facsimile of fun for the right price?

One of Blackpool's attractions proved nothing out of the ordinary for someone from Walsall. To extend the holiday season, every year since 1879 the resort puts up six miles of illuminated streetlights and tableaus. The big switch on still happens in September, and the festival extends well into autumn. At the time, Walsall had its version of the Blackpool lights. The 'Illuminations' in the town's large Arboretum was, like Blackpool, a free spectacle. It all began in September 1951 as part of the town's celebrations for the Festival of Britain, and its success encouraged the council to repeat the event annually. Whereas Blackpool's display centred on its Promenade, Walsall used the trees as coat hangers for coloured lights next to floodlit flowerbeds and illuminated water jets on the ornamental lake[48].

When my sons go on holiday, they always get in touch by text, usually with a photograph or video clip attached. Increasingly, video calls involve them spinning the camera around to show where they are staying and to look at the scene they are viewing. Such instantaneous communication was unheard of then. Being away on holiday meant having to buy postcards early in the week. Mom would write them on the beach, and they would be posted no later than Monday in order that friends and relatives would get the card before we returned home. Normally card writing involved a brief comment on the weather, the fact that you are enjoying your holiday and 'wishing you were here'. Postcards were a key ingredient of holidays and at their height sold at the rate of sixteen million a year. The cards themselves tended to fall into three main categories. First there was the decorative type, possibly an illustrated map of the area. Second there was the colour photograph type, sometimes of a very mundane local landmark. These always came complete with artificially enhanced blue cloudless skies. Then there would be the cartoon type with its 'humorous' message. Cards featured thin, balding, hen-pecked men, fat older ladies and busty young women and came complete with a sexual innuendo. During the fifties, the government even felt it necessary to intervene to curb the worst excesses of this form of vulgarity, but still the cards persisted and sold in big numbers. Just as miniature flags and donkey rides have now given way to paddle boards and windsurfers, so *Facetime*, *Zoom* and *Skype* have all but replaced postcards. The

---

48 The event ceased in 2008, because of mounting financial losses and the negative environmental impact on the Arboretum.

idea of writing postcards as a way of reassuring relatives that all is well is now as outdated as using a Victorian bathing machine.

For my family, the idea of a foreign holiday was out of the question, it was for someone else altogether, a different class of person. Like eating a meal in a restaurant, it was not something we did. To suggest flying away on holiday was about as realistic as suggesting a space flight[49]. Yet in magazines and television programmes we saw people like film star Brigitte Bardot or artist Picasso enjoying the blazing French Riviera sun. Could anyone I know experience the sunshine these celebrities did? For some ordinary families change was coming. Foreign travel may have been the preserve of the monied upper classes, but war meant that ordinary working-class men serving in the military had been introduced to other lands and experiences. The idea of a foreign package holiday, though in its infancy, was gaining leverage thanks to weekly saving schemes. Package holidays targeted Spain, which was still living under the firm, and at times brutal, dictatorship of General Franco[50]. Overheard conversations in shops and in bus queues confirmed that a holiday in the sun was a realistic possibility now for people like us. Those enticed by the prospect could return from destinations with exotic names like Benidorm and Costa Brava, with tales of cocktails and places where you could get *Watney's Red Barrel* beer. Strange knickknacks like pendants, pictures of foreign landscapes and fluffy donkeys wearing sombreros evidenced experiencing something quite different. One of my Sunday school teachers and the Simms family were the only people I knew who took advantage of a package holiday. Mom and Dad were never tempted and disliked sitting in the sun anyway. Holidays, happy days?

---

49  I had my first passport when I was a married twenty-four years old!

50  Spain reverted to being a democracy following the death of Franco in 1975. Picasso exiled himself from his Spanish homeland because of the brutality of the dictatorship.

# Chapter Nine

## *Old folks*

I knew my maternal grandparents well. Nan and Grandad lived within walking distance and just down from the church we attended as a family. We would see them several times a week, and they joined us every Christmas Day and for some family holidays. Being in their company set Dad off complaining about how irritating and troublesome they were. The truth was they were no trouble at all, and Dad being irritated was far from being a rare occurrence.

I loved them. They offered a richness to my life as a kid with their clothes, habits and stories pointing to a strange, lost world of the distant past. At the time, Nan and Grandad and their siblings seemed much older than being fifty-something. There was a weariness about them that made you think that they were incredibly old. Children are notoriously bad when guessing the age of an adult, but I felt that I had the oldest grandparents in the world. They may have called themselves Mr and Mrs Bryant, but the pair may as well have been Mr and Mrs Methuselah. I suppose that Grandad had earned his living on the factory floor, suffered from hardening of the arteries, lived through two world wars and the Great Depression and much more, which would age anyone.

Apart from using expressions that no one else did (like the s-hole to signify the chimney), they also seemed to have phrases that should have died out following the English Civil War, for instance:

'What time is it, Bill?'

'It's five and twenty past two.'

'What time does the bus run?'

'Oh, it arrives at five and twenty to the hour.'

Nan was small, walked with a distinctive roll of the shoulders and had almost sculptured white hair. Suffering from a combination of asthma and anxiety, she never worked after marrying. The couple started married life together, sharing a Walsall council house with her widowed mother. By the time they become grandparents they lived in their own home, a council owned prefab.

Nan smelt of *TCP antiseptic* fluid thanks to years of daily gargling. There must be health benefits to the practice, but I am at a loss to think what they might be. What I am certain of is that it had the effect of stripping her of her sense of smell and taste as well as adding a distinctive fragrance to her clothing, her home, and its contents. As well as the smell, her prefab had a huge bed with multiple pillows and a fascinating dressing table where lavender-smelling bottles and bath cubes were placed unopened and proudly on display, representing reminders of Christmas and birthdays past.

Nan's determination to consume *TCP* was matched only by her determination to back her daughter in all matters. So, when Mom was telling her anything, she was the model of active listening. She nodded vigorously and attempted to join in by anticipating and repeating the end of a key sentence. For some reason, she believed that one of her roles as a grandparent was to contribute when her grandsons were taking a telling off. 'Yes, that's right.' 'Your Mom is right.' 'Well, if you had listened to your Mom ...', and so on.

When she was with her sisters, Nan became 'our Sarah Ann,' abbreviated to Sar-ann. I met Nan's older sisters, May and Lil, several times. These were both formidable, no-nonsense types and were very distant to the point of almost ignoring my existence completely. I suppose this was a legacy of an upbringing when children should be 'seen and not heard'. Nan's younger sister Rene was different, she was friendly, had time for me and seemed more like a half-sister to Mom.

Nan also had two brothers, both of whom served in the army during the ridiculously named Great War[51]. She once told me

---

51 The name given to the carnage of the 1914–1918 First World War. Estimates of casualties vary but it is likely to be of the order of twenty million deaths with a similar number of wounded.

of a spoon her mother treasured that was split from the bowl to halfway down the handle. This had taken the impact of an enemy bullet while resting in one of her son's breast pockets. The mundane had become vital, and the sacrifice of the spoon had saved the sacrifice of yet another life, another son, brother, and husband.

I visited one of Nan's brothers on a single memorable occasion. I am not sure if he was the 'spoon' brother or the other one, either way, his name was Joe. In the run-up to Christmas, Mom decided it would be a good idea to take Nan and Lil to see him. This meant a ride out in the car, but the prospect did not strike me as being likely to be very entertaining. How wrong I was, it offered an experience that lives with me to this day.

Joe lived nine or so miles away in Burntwood. Although Walsall was classified as being part of the same county, the territory we covered was unfamiliar and alien. With our breath producing mist on the inside of the car windows, we journeyed through a far more countrified version of Staffordshire. We saw open fields, trees and hedges picturesquely dusted in December frost. This was a timeless, tranquil landscape that came complete with a seasonal sprinkle of white. It was as if this part of the world had been shielded from the coming of the industrial revolution and had looked the same for years.

Eventually, arriving at our destination, we pulled up in the grounds of an imposing building called St. Matthews. Once inside, we waited in a dining hall capable of accommodating hundreds. Sat behind one of the many *Formica* topped tables it had the feel of prison visiting time. After a while Joe was brought to join us. He was wearing a strange combination of nightwear and day clothes. His slippers and pyjama bottoms were topped off with a shirt, cardigan, and old checked jacket. I was impressed that he was uninhibited by the way he was dressed in a public place. I do not remember him saying much. His eyes and thoughts were elsewhere. While the others engaged in conversation, I fixed my look on Joe. Like me, he was a conscripted observer rather than a participant in the discussions that were going on. Strong medication may or may not have accounted for his lack of engagement. He displayed an ability to chew humbugs (which Lil had produced from a huge handbag) and smoke a cigarette at the same time. He had carefully rolled the cigarette while seeming oblivious to the fact that Mom, Nan, and Lil were chatting at the same table.

Then it happened. He pushed the tobacco tin and *Rizla* papers to one side and began shuffling about in his right jacket pocket. He then produced another small tin, which he placed deliberately on the table. I noticed that his fingers were gnarled and inflexibly puffy, and some were stained brown with nicotine. Despite sausages for fingers, he applied surgical precision to carefully open the tin and pull out a carefully judged quantity of the mystery substance. Using his middle and forefingers as expert instruments, he placed a quantity of the substance on the back of the first finger and thumb of his left hand, raised it to his left nostril, sniffed in a deliberate, extended fashion, then repeated the procedure with his right nostril. I looked at the others around the table. No one was trying to stop him putting the contents of a cigarette up his nose. After a few seconds he stared into space and sneezed distractedly. As he did so, his visitors broke off from their conversation to chorus 'bless you'. Then he reached again for his pocket and eventually unearthed a once white handkerchief to dab his nose. Nothing was said about the incident.

I had just witnessed snuff taking. I was appalled, astounded, but somehow attracted to the practice. Smoking went on around me all the while. I had now observed another method of welcoming nicotine into the human body. This time the chosen method did not impact too much on anyone else. Snuff taking was hugely popular during the nineteenth century, more popular than smoking even. Then marketeers attempted to convince the adult population of the convenience and elegance of smoking perfectly formed filter-ready rolled cigarettes as an alternative. Joe had ignored the marketeers' message. For Joe, snuff taking and cigarette rolling were welcome, time-consuming distractions he could engage in and control. They represented his comfort blanket in the depleted impersonal world he now found himself in.

Joe was doubtless traumatised by the War and the 'land fit for heroes[52]' he was promised became instead an institutionalised life that could hardly have been of his choosing. His indulgences with tobacco were small, deliberate pleasures he could enjoy. Ideas on caring for those with mental ill health have changed considerably since this time. Terms like post-traumatic stress disorder did not exist, and the mental ghosts of what Joe endured and witnessed during the War were either unrecognised or ignored. I am not sure whether St. Matthews was a lunatic asylum or a hospital, but it had the feel of both. It was a truly awful place. I was grateful I never had to go back there again.

William (Bill) Bryant, Grandad, was a source of fascination because he failed to conform to the 'rules' that my brother and I had to follow. He did not use the seat belt in the car[53], instead he just pulled the belt over his belly and held it there. After going to the loo, he made a point of not washing his hands. He emptied spent tea leaves from the teapot down the toilet, banging the pot on the porcelain before flushing the chain. He would also belch unapologetically, often muttering 'manners' to himself rather than addressing his unwilling audience with 'beg your pardon'. He also used cutlery in the 'wrong hands' on account of his left-handedness. He told me how his schoolteachers had tried to 'cure' him of this affliction when writing. His

---

52 In 1918 the then Prime Minister David Lloyd George set the country the task of making it a land fit for heroes when rebuilding society after the First World War.

53 Wearing a seatbelt may come as second nature nowadays. The requirement to fit belts was not introduced until 1968 and the compulsory wearing of belts was not introduced until as late as 1983.

left-sided bias however allowed him to box southpaw and play left back for the local church side in his youth.

Today men might shave their heads by choice, and some, such as football manager Pep Guardiola, might look cool as a result. This was not the case when I was young. Baldness was involuntary and decidedly uncool. Bill was bald but had thick eyebrows as some sort of consolation. He also had an enormous belly, which was accentuated by trousers that extended a good way up his torso, almost reaching his chest. The effect was achieved with a scaffold of secure trouser braces. (He may have had his braces, but his grandsons had elasticated multi-coloured belts with a snake for a buckle.)

Dentists and toothpaste companies nowadays stress the need to protect enamel on teeth. When I was a child, the emphasis was instead on avoiding fillings. So, while we desisted from sweets and brushed our teeth religiously, Grandad seemed to get along fine with his missing front teeth and two bottom-row tooth stubs. While I had to concern myself with combing my hair and brushing my teeth in a morning, he had none of these burdens.

Born in 1901, Bill was fortunate to be too young for service in the First World War, and too old for the Second World War. He may have escaped the armed service, but he, like Nan, had to live through and survive the Spanish flu epidemic of 1918. The epidemic offered an echo of what later generations would encounter a century later with the Coronavirus (COVID-19) outbreak. It has been said that history never repeats itself, but it does rhyme[54]. The similarities are obvious, but the main difference is that the earlier epidemic proved more deadly, infecting one in three of the world's population and killing millions.

By the time I knew him, he lacked mobility, and a medical condition forced him to retire prematurely from work. He spent long hours shuffling from room to room, hardly ever going outside

---

54  Attributed to American writer and humourist Mark Twain 1835–1910 but most likely an old saying.

until he became completely housebound. Sitting with him as a child, he taught me to play both draughts and card games. He could be found reading his daily newspaper or filing his fingernails. Freed from his job as a metal polisher, he was now able to allow his battered fingers and nails to recover. Apart from gnarled hands, the job left him with the legacy of a crooked nose, caused when a brass port hole cover dropped onto it while he was polishing its base.

Bill was someone who found it hard to cope with change and the march of technology. This evidenced itself in several ways. He continued to listen to football results on the radio rather than watch the scores come in on the television. He preferred to toast bread on a fork in front of the electric fire rather than use the grill or a toaster. When faced with a tea bag for the first time, he cut into it, releasing the tea into a pot so that he could make a cuppa in the usual way.

He was a Brummie and had a sister called Sissie, who still lived in the city. The six of us crammed into the car to visit her on two occasions, both wet Sunday afternoons. On the first occasion, Sissie was living in a back-to-back terraced house with husband Bert. The house had a dark, comfortable feel and a small narrow garden (where Bert was cultivating vegetables arranged in neat rows) that led to an outside toilet. The next time we visited the outdoor loo and garden were gone. The couple now resided in a high-rise paradise complete with artificial light as bright as any lighthouse. Ascending to the tenth floor by lift, we arrived at Sissie's new home without seeing another soul. The only evidence that others lived in the same building were the empty milk bottles and door mats outside front doors. Sissie went to some lengths to say how much better it was to live where they now did. It is good that she approved, because the whole setup seemed soulless and imprisoning. I doubt that the tower block I visited that day is still standing.

I never knew another set of grandparents. Dad's mother was long deceased, and his father, Job, was in poor health and living in Bedfordshire with Aunty Margaret. Although named on

Mom and Dad's marriage certificate, Job did not figure in any of their wedding photographs. The reason for this was quite straightforward, he was not there. Few parents would view another activity more important than attending their only son's wedding, yet no one who knew Job was in any way surprised by his 'no show'. Job had his own way of doing things.

After the death of her mother, Dad's elder sister Daisy stepped into her role, while Job, when not at work, was playing 'Jack the Lad' in the pubs around the town centre. Job was a great raconteur, and his stories and experiences were endlessly repeated by those who knew him. He also made good use of his withering sarcasm. His usual targets were those in positions of authority, especially if they were pompous or officious. Those hearing these exchanges were hugely amused and entertained, while his targets were often left embarrassed and humiliated.

During the First World War, Job saw service in the trenches of Europe as part of the Liverpool regiment. Job was responsible for operating one of the machine guns. On one fateful day it became apparent that the enemy was about to prevail, so he quickly swapped his jacket and cap with a dead soldier from a different regiment. His quick thinking saved his life as minutes later the post was seized. Others from his regiment were unceremoniously executed on the spot by a bullet from a German officer's gun. Imprisonment in a prisoner-of-war camp followed, but the story did not end there. Job somehow managed to escape and was on the run for several days, living off turnips that were growing in the fields round about. Eventually he decided to ask for directions so he could make it to a neutral country. Seeing a railway station, he asked for help. Unfortunately, the person he selected to speak to happened to be an off-duty German officer. Job was returned to the prison camp, where he remained for the duration of the war.

Back home in 1918, he found work in a steel mill in Walsall. It was a gruelling job, and breaks between shifts involved the consumption of up to six pints of dark mild in a local pub. Mild had a lower alcoholic strength than bitter and helped snake the thirst of the sweaty steelworkers. More importantly, its sweetness helped replenish lost body sugars. Job took responsibility for a team producing as many 'good' lengths of steel as possible during the working week. A system operated whereby the company paid chargehands for the number of completed unblemished lengths and left the onward distribution of cash to them. Job had a particular method of doing this. After bathing to rid himself of grime from a hard week's graft, he would put on his Sunday best outfit and head into the town centre. Booted and suited, his outfit was completed with an impressive pocket watch and a wad of bank notes. He would then position himself in the snug of the George Hotel 'early doors'. Doubtless receiving drinks from his team, he would decide on how best to divvy up the pay. His return home was very much later after a long liquid lunch, laughter, storytelling, and socialising.

I have an early memory of visiting him on a single occasion. The involuntary inhaling of mustard gas during the War and hard manual work had taken its toll on his body. He spent the last years of his life bed-bound and nursed by Margaret. Mom and Dad must have decided to visit him shortly before his death in 1961. Tim was a baby at the time, and I may not have even been school age. I do however distinctly remember being led into a bedroom where he lay. The bed was huge, and the bedsheets smelt of starch and ill health. Propped up by huge white pillows, an old man with a fine head of white hair and sparkling eyes tried to engage me in conversation. I was told afterwards that he told me that I was a healthy, strong-looking lad and one day might grow up to be a champion boxer, just like his own grandfather, the Tipton Slasher.

Tipton is typical of a Black Country town built around an effective canal network and comprising a community bound by hard work, poor living conditions and their sporting interests. The thing that distinguishes the town from others is that it has produced at least two sporting legends. Steve Bull was born there in 1965 and went on to play for England and spend thirteen years as the star player and record goal scorer for Wolverhampton

Wanderers. A century earlier it was also the birthplace of William Perry. Known as the Tipton Slasher, he was prize fighting champion of England for two periods between 1850 and 1857 and one of the greatest bare-knuckle fighters of all time. Born around 1819, Perry graduated to prize fighting after an early career working on the barges of Tipton. A remarkable fighter with a distinctive slashing motion (hence the nickname), he became champion of England while owning the Fountain, a local pub. Today, the Fountain overlooks the canal and a statue of one of the Black Country's most famous sons.

So, Job's grandfather was William Perry making the pugilist my great, great grandfather? This made me a direct descendant of a Black Country-born and bred hero. My birth may have been in a sanitised corner of 1950s suburbia, but I could claim pure Black Country DNA. This thought set my imagination racing as a child. In this pre-internet search era, I began collecting what information I could on my ancestor from newspaper and magazine articles that came my way.

# Chapter Ten

## *Yew Tree People*

Mom and Dad had plenty of friends who lived on the estate. They included neighbours and parents with children around the same age as their boys, or people they got to know through the church we attended as a family. Close friends included the Pheasants and the Houghtons. Arthur and Jane Pheasant lived in nearby Almond Avenue, and I knew their younger children, Michael and Elaine, quite well through get-togethers and Sunday School. Elsie and Tom Houghton lived around the corner, and we once shared a holiday with them and their family, including Ian who was a classmate who joined in most football kickabouts I was involved in.

Mom loved company and once a month there was a meeting of the 'young wives' group[55] at the church, which offered her a rare night out. After the meeting and walking back to the estate, there would be gaggles of giggling, guffawing women with names like Phyllis, Muriel, Beryl, and Joyce. The raucous conversations would then continue over a cup of tea at someone's home. If Mom found something funny, she would go into fits of uncontrollable laughter. When she brought her friends back, I would lie in bed listening with fascination to the loud conversation and hysterical laughter. After ten minutes or so of this, Dad would not be best pleased. If he felt the get-together was going on too long, he would go upstairs and then reappear in his pyjamas (with working trousers over the top) to make cocoa for himself, sighing deeply as he did so. Obviously, this was the prompt for further noise and hilarity.

---

55 A non-conformist version of the Church of England's Women's Institute.

Mom had two particularly good friends in Mrs Skinner and Mrs Simms. I was the grateful recipient of selection boxes at Christmas and chocolate eggs at Easter from them both. Mom discouraged the eating of chocolates and sweets ('otherwise you will need fillings'), so this was a welcome treat. Mrs Simms also bought a few fireworks for me in the week before bonfire night. Both women had interesting households and were married to men with hobbies that were taken to near obsessional lengths.

Mom encouraged us to call Mrs Skinner 'Aunty', and I never knew her forename[56]. Older than Mom, she was a caring lady who took time over me. I was possibly special to her as she was there supporting Mom at my birth. She lived next door but one in an identical house to ours and had two children of her own, Hayley and Michael. Both were older than me, so I did not have that much to do with them.

I understand that her husband Jack was classified as 'missing presumed dead' during the war but eventually returned home to find things not exactly as he had pictured them. There was an unexpected resident in his house called Karl. Karl, who had luxurious white hair and piercing blue eyes, was a former prisoner of war (POW) who had failed to return to Germany[57]. Unlike every other household in the street, 22 Lilac Avenue did not fit into the normal nuclear family template. Instead, three adults and two children co-existed.

In an era obsessed with the possibility of 'reds under the bed' and clandestine spying operations, it would be possible to fantasise that Karl was an undercover agent. If he was, he must have been the worst mole the Soviets ever had. He had a distinctive Teutonic look, and a thick accent that stood out amongst the Black Country voices all around him. Then there was the subject matter of his reports back to the other side of the Iron Curtain. The happenings on Yew Tree Estate and the operation

---

56 Which was normally referred to as a Christian name at this time.
57 25,000 German POWs opted to remain in Britain after the War.

of the sewerage works would surely seem too mundane for the Kremlin back in Moscow?

More realistically, Karl's presence drew speculation of a different sort. Mom would not hear of any gossip or talk by 'dirty-minded' neighbours because she 'knew' Mrs Skinner. Karl was a lodger who was only taken in by Mrs Skinner because of her big heart. End of story. Quite apart from Karl's status as a lodger, there were of course other questions. Questions like, was Karl a threat to Jack's marriage and how could two men who had been at war with one another a few short years earlier peacefully live under the same roof? As a child I never gave these matters any thought, I just accepted things as they were.

In an era when there was only one live televised football game a year, the significance of winning the FA Cup final was great. The year I was born[58], Manchester City triumphed, and the hero of the final was their goalkeeper, who was severely injured during the game. This was a time before substitutes were permitted, but rather than leave the field, he chose to play on and made several decent saves despite his obvious discomfort. A few days later it took two sets of X-rays to reveal that he had a broken neck. The brave goalkeeper was Bert Trautmann and football writers voted him player of the season. The remarkable thing about Trautmann was that, like Karl he was a German POW who had settled in Britain. Trautmann was formerly a Nazi, and when Manchester City first signed him there were protests organised by supporters and the local Jewish community. Trautmann's obvious ability, bravery and faithful fifteen years' service to his club won some of his critics over. What is indisputable is that Trautmann led a remarkable life and became the only person to be awarded both the Iron Cross (for bravery in battle) and an OBE (for work on Anglo-German relations). Karl, by comparison, just got on with integrating into the Yew Tree estate culture.

---

58  1956.

One August evening in 1961, the ideological divide between the two great political power blocs of the time was given physical expression in the homeland that Karl and Trautmann once shared. The Berlin Wall was formed out of huge three-metre slabs of concrete separating the west and east sides of the city. The physical division symbolised the reality of the divide between two different world views. Ordinary Germans lost their lives trying to cross the wall, some simply attempting to return home having been trapped on the 'wrong' side of the city.

Dad had picked up conversational German, having served in Austria with the army, and enjoyed his discussions with Karl. Dad was also one of the people who signed the required paperwork paving the way to Karl's eventual British naturalisation.

Jack Skinner was a modest, unassuming sort who taught both my parents to drive and get full driving licences. Jack had one consuming passion in life, something that gave a release from the mundane and helped numb memories of his wartime experiences. His passion was Walsall Football Club. He never missed a home game at Fellows Park, travelled to some away matches and spoke with authority on all things Walsall FC. He had an encyclopaedic knowledge of players and games. He also had the kudos of being on speaking terms with a Walsall player of the period, Nick Atthey, who also lived on the estate in a house that was rented to him by the club.

Mom was a resourceful person. She was proficient at knitting, repairing, and making the odd item of clothing for her young family. Her most ambitious project was making page boy outfits styled on Scottish national dress for her two sons when they were enlisted as page boys at a family friend's wedding (Dad was also best man). Regrettably, she was unable to see for herself the results of her endeavours as she contracted influenza and was laid up in bed as the wedding took place. She once enrolled in a sewing and dress-making evening class at the school, and it was there that she met Phyllis Simms. Phyllis lived with her husband Arthur and children Barbara, Graham, and Gillian on the other side of the estate. I liked the family.

They were generous, welcoming, and kind. They were different, more Black Country, more blue collar, more 'West Bromwich'. When Mom referred to going 'down the town', she meant Walsall town centre. When Mrs Simms used the phrase 'up the town', she meant West Bromwich town centre.

Graham was older than me and I was impressed by the fact that he was allowed to eat banana sandwiches as a snack and repair his bike tyre in the kitchen sink. Without an older brother, Graham was my only source of hand-me-downs. I remember inheriting a red and grey dressing gown, a Life Boys uniform, a model castle, and some metal soldiers. I also read a steady supply of *Eagle* and *Boys Own* comics once he had finished with them. The comics themselves were quite serious by nature, with an emphasis on education more than entertainment. Highlights for me were cutaway pictures showing the working of, say, a train, a galleon, or a battleship and the adventures of Dan Dare, 'pilot of the future'.

Dan Dare's fictional adventures paled into insignificance when compared to some of the heroic tales of real-life victories during the Second World War. None more so than the exploits of the Seventh Armoured Division or desert rats who helped defeat the more experienced German Afrika Korps, led by the most successful and celebrated enemy general, 'the desert fox', Erwin Rommel. Mom said Arthur had been a desert rat during the war and had seen some awful things. Things he never spoke of. It was quite possible that he never spoke of these things because no one asked him. Either way, he was an unlikely-looking war hero. Life outside the forces meant family life and demanding manual work, including that of a foundry labourer. Sometime later, when Dad became a works manager at a steel stockholder in Walsall, he was able to offer Arthur less physical work in a cleaner environment. Later, Dad also took Barbara's husband John onto the workforce.

Arthur was a small, friendly sort, very deaf, with thick glasses and slicked-back hair flattened to his head. He always wore jackets with cuffs that threatened to swallow his knuckles. The most remarkable thing about Arthur however was his passion for his car. I cannot remember what make the object of his passion was, but it was big and had gleaming black paintwork. Huge indicators popped out of the side of it like illuminated flags when signalling[59]. Curiously, the car contained 'running boards' down the side and the opportunity to hand crank the engine into life just below the pressed tin black and white number plate. The smart interior boasted leather upholstery and a walnut-coloured dashboard with switches and dials that contributed to a far more impressive cockpit than that depicted in Dan Dare's plane. Rather than the usual separate seats at the front, there was a bench seat instead. The car was his pride and joy, and he lavished much time and effort on it.

On visits to their home, Arthur could often be found with his head buried under the bonnet of the mechanical monster. The car was washed and waxed every weekend, and the chrome never gleamed so much as shone. The glass was perfectly clean and, like the paintwork, completely smear-free. When rain threatened to upset this arrangement, then Arthur would leather the rain spots off in the garage. If the tyres were looking dirty, the car would be jacked up, and they would be removed one by one to be scrubbed in the sink and then 'blacked'. Arthur's obsession with his motor extended to the fuel it consumed. He insisted on only using Mobil petrol, believing every other brand to be somehow inferior and this might hinder the smooth running of his treasured possession. What he would have made of modern-day electric cars and dual fuel motors is anybody's guess.

Many years later, Phyllis and Arthur were guests at my wedding. Arthur doubtless gave his car a complete clean for the occasion. Mrs Skinner, Jack, and Karl were also guests.

Jack died a short time after my wedding. If he could have planned his demise, it would have been on the Fellows Park pitch

---

59 Despite this obvious signal to fellow motorists and pedestrians the driving test of the period required the driver to use hand signals.

playing for his beloved club. In the event he died on the terraces following a heart attack. Eerily, his image appeared in the background of an action shot in the *Walsall Observer* as part of the report on the last game Jim watched. The caption underneath confirmed the minute of the match that the picture had been taken, which was, at most, minutes before he died.

In terms of Karl's homeland, the Berlin Wall was still standing until 1989, twenty-eight years after its construction. The dismantling of the wall signalling the fall of the Soviet Union itself. Karl never returned to Germany even after this, not even for a visit. The reason as to why this might be gives rise to various possibilities, some more intriguing than others. The more mundane explanation is of course that he was from a part of the country that became East Germany and did not relish the prospect of living under communism. When the wall fell, he had lost any interest in paying a visit. Alternatively, he may have had a wife or a life he never wanted to return to in his homeland. I will never know.

# Chapter Eleven

## *On the seventh day*

Nowadays changing working patterns are on the increase with arrangements such as homeworking and the use of self-managed flexi-hours. Employment contracts now concentrate on the achievement of outputs and outcomes rather than times of hourly attendance. For many businesses, the working week of nine until five, Monday to Friday, has been set aside in the quest to become more flexible and remain competitive. Practices such as these have evolved organisation by organisation over time. Rethinking the traditional working week however is not a new concept. Following the French revolution over 230 years ago, some novel ideas were put into practice, including a redrawing of the traditional Gregorian calendar. Distancing itself from past religious influences, a decimalised system was introduced. The new calendar was used by Napoleon Bonaparte and the French government for a mere twelve years before falling into disuse due to lack of popularity. Little wonder, for the ordinary worker this meant that a day of rest fell every tenth rather than seventh day. Even citizens of a revolution felt a need to mirror the biblical example of God by resting on the seventh day!

The Sundays I knew as a child were unlike any other day of the week. For the residents of 26 Lilac Avenue, the day had a familiar, mostly comforting pattern. This was the day that Dad became involved in the kitchen first thing in the morning. He would burn bacon rashers to such a degree that they became black and crunchy and resembled a discarded by-product of a pork scratchings factory. Mostly we avoided Dad's sabbath burnt offering and ate what Mom put in front of us for breakfast. After this we would walk the short distance across the Common to 'our' church kitted out in our 'Sunday best' clothes. Treating this day as, if not a day of rest, then a 'different' day was not unique to our household. Everyone in the country knew Sunday was different for good reason. That reason was not so much religious zeal as legislation. The Shops Act of 1950[60] meant that buying and selling on Sunday was effectively illegal. There were certain exceptions, of course, that could legally be purchased, but essentially the legislation tried to force the country to observe the Sunday as a day of rest. There was no such thing as popping to the shops for the item that had just run out! Shopkeepers everywhere pulled their shutters down for the day. Unlike other Western European countries, there were no sporting events on a Sunday either. There was a complete rest from work, school, sport, consumerism and everything else that went on the other six days of the week!

To modern day thinking the imposition of a day of rest for the citizens' own good smacks of living in an overprotective, interfering nanny state. There were many more instances of nannyism, most passively accepted. The most bizarre example took place between 1953 and 1957 when the Government once more felt it was acting in a socially responsible way by interfering in TV programming. The government stipulated that there would be a break in coverage every night between 6pm and 7pm when television screens would simply go blank. The downtime they had created (nicknamed 'toddlers' truce') represented an opportunity for responsible parents to put their children to bed at the right time.

Without other weekday distractions, the opportunity to make Sunday special was embraced by our household, with food and church being dominant themes. This was a day of rituals like wearing your best clothes, going to church, and eating roast dinner and tinned salmon sandwiches for tea. These rituals helped to mark the passing of one week and the start of another.

Delves Baptist church was well attended by both families from the estate and those who lived on the other side of the

---

60 The law stayed on the statute books until 1994. The first Sunday game of League Football was in 1974. This was as a response to the oil crisis and the miners' strike. The morning kick off avoided using floodlights.

Common in the local Delves area. The church itself was a modest but welcoming affair. The Spartan nature of the building could have been personally approved of by Oliver Cromwell himself. Shunning stained glass, pews and candles, the building had the reformist modesty of white emulsion walls, sensible stacking chairs and the possibility of sticky cakes at church socials. Next to the church were a couple of former military wooden huts used by Sunday school on Sundays and by other church groups during the week. I got used to the familiar pattern of church worship (notices and welcome; hymn; children's address; hymn; go into Sunday school; return to see Mom and Dad at the end).

Back home after the Sunday service there was the enticing smell of a roast dinner cooking, which Mom presided over. Meanwhile Dad caught up on paperwork from work in the lounge while listening to 'two-way family favourites' on the radio. The hugely popular programme was broadcast on the BBC Light (entertainment) Programme and linked families to relatives in West Germany and elsewhere in the world as part of British Forces Posted Overseas (BFPO). Without the benefit of modern-day technology, hearing families greeting loved ones in real time was ground-breaking. A song was chosen by each family, and a Frank Sinatra track was chosen most weeks, which Dad loved to whistle and hum along to.

Following a heavy lunch, Tim and I would make a return trip to the church for afternoon Sunday School classes aimed at younger children. As we got older, we would just slump in the lounge before the television set. By the mid-sixties it was possible to see highlights of a midland football match played the previous day on the commercial TV show *Star Soccer*. This was the best substitute there was for watching a live football match. There was only one match selected, so if the match chosen was a dull goalless draw, then it was a 'tough watch'. While all this was going on, Dad would read the Sunday newspaper which contained supplements and magazines which formed a circle around his feet. After a while Mom would then begin making Sunday tea. Tins containing salmon, fruit in syrup and evaporated milk might be opened for the occasion. These items only saw light of day on a Sunday. It was an unwritten rule that this was 'Sunday food'.

Much later I brought my girlfriend (now wife) home for Sunday tea. She was surprised at how much of the food was made by Mom, including homemade jam, quince jelly, cake, and bread. This I just took for granted. To my shame, I never acknowledged or thanked Mom for the enormous effort that went into us all overeating together on a Sunday. Instead, I would joke that the bread tasted more like cake than the cake (which was not true anyway). Whatever Sunday was, it was never a day of rest for Mom.

A.N. Wilson, who is today a full-blown apologist, has written about his non-religious upbringing. Born in the fifties, he observed that *'like most educated people in Britain and Northern Europe ... I have grown up in a culture that is overwhelmingly secular and anti-religious'*. That was clearly true for Wilson and possibly the majority, but it was never my experience. I only became aware of the wider culture when I reached senior school age and went to school away from the Estate. I may have been born and raised in a post-Christian, increasingly secular country, but I existed in the warm bubble of a subculture where church attendance seemed the normal thing to do. A sizeable proportion of my school classmates either attended the church I did or a Roman Catholic church. Several friends I knew from the street joined me at both the morning and afternoon Sunday school.

It seems a curious thing that having been under compulsion to attend school five days a week any child would want to voluntarily undertake further schooling. Sunday school sixties style, however, was not really like school at all, it was far less formal. There would be a bible story that would form the basis of craft, activities, songs, and a chat, then there would be things like the Sunday school anniversary or the Christmas presentation to prepare for. Nationally, Sunday school attendance was huge in the mid-nineteenth century, but a hundred years later was in steep decline. Not that you would detect this from the healthy attendance at Delves Baptist Sunday school.

The earlier national appetite for Sunday schools is best understood in the context of the time. During the Industrial Revolution, factory and mill owners mercilessly exploited children for their labour. In 1802, the first modest legislative restrictions limited the number of hours a child could work per day to twelve! In practice this meant that children spent most of their waking hours labouring in factories six days a week, often legally clocking up seventy-two hours. Christian philanthropists believed that education and literacy was the only way to free working-class children from this life of exploitation and drudgery. As Sunday was the only available time, Sunday schools grew as part of a church's wider activities. Encouraged by their parents, many children eagerly embraced the offer of free education. Inevitably the emphasis was upon religious education, with the Bible being used as a reading book and source for copying out passages of scripture. In addition to the schooling, other highlights for the children included prize givings, parades and picnics. The nature of the Sunday school I knew had evolved by then.

I have a friend, Barry, who also attended an afternoon Sunday School class as a child. Indeed he was awarded certificates for having the best attendance for several years running. The strange thing was that his parents were 'not very religious' and never went to church. They were however unyieldingly insistent on him keeping up his attendance. This remained a source of confusion for Barry well into adult life until he reflected on how small their family home was and how wafer-thin the walls were. It is likely that while many children engaged in Sunday school activities, their parents observed their own Sabbath rituals between the bedsheets.

I willingly attended church or Sunday school when I was young. The church had much to commend it. I loved the fairs and church socials with the dancing to awful music and laughing at corny routines contributed by members of the congregation. There were simple pleasures like buying cheap, tasteless items at 'bring and buy' events and eating food we did not normally eat at home (every family would bring a plate of either savoury or sweet food for sharing).

There was the early Monday evening *Life Boys* meeting, aimed at junior school-age lads. *Life Boys* were to the *Boys Brigade* what the *Cubs* were to the *Scouts*. The rival *Scouts* organisation seemed considerably more appealing with its award of multiple badges, bonfires, and its woggle neckwear. While our rivals grabbed the headlines with their boisterous jamborees and 'bob a job'[61] fund-raising weeks, we contented ourselves with games, football, and uniform inspections. Like Sunday schools, these uniformed organisations were far less popular than they had been in previous generations and suffered from declining numbers. This was just as well; the earlier Hitler youth movement had cast a shadow over other uniformed child organisations that followed it. If the *Boys Brigade* football team were short of players, some of the older life boys would be enlisted to make up the numbers. This involved wearing an oversized team kit and then facing a rival brigade who might mercilessly run up a double-digit victory. The age limit was meant to be up to fifteen years old, but I remember facing lads who had shaver's rash and arms thicker than my thighs.

At special times in my life, I have known feelings where the veil between heaven and earth appeared thin. What I mean by this is that I have experienced something special in acts of worship or have been caught out by the wonder of the natural world. I never experienced feelings like this at Delves Baptist Church. Instead, I was accepted into a community of people who attended a weekly extended version of a school assembly. I encountered genuine, gentle, and well-meaning people who exuded a sense of decency and lived ordered, honest lives. They had found a place where they could worship a higher being they believed in. I suppose they were trying to work out the relationship between God and the individual, and what each person's place and purpose on earth was.

---

61 The agreement to undertake a task for the payment of a 'bob', the nickname for a shilling (5p today).

It was here that I encountered same-sex couples for the first time. Their relationships were accepted without comment by everyone in the congregation with Quaker type tolerance. The fact that they were 'out' was rare by the standards of the day and a credit to the attitude and inclusiveness of the church. One couple lived just around the corner in the Delves area. Marjorie was a bit scatterbrained but very friendly. Her partner, Florrie Hale, was the Superintendent Sunday school leader who signed the certificates that were stuck in the front of prize-giving books. She wore silk scarves and called everyone 'dear'. What impressed me most about her was that when she lit the birthday candles, she would strike a match on the sole of her shoe. There was also a younger lesbian couple who did not share a home. Eventually they chose to emigrate, possibly because it was easier to make a clean break from their families and to live together. Family pressure and fear of rejection can combine to become powerful forces.

I remember two ministers who served the church while I was there. The first was Norman Parkes, who tried to compensate for his meagre salary by eating his own body weight at church get-togethers. He had a wife and family. When he moved on to another circuit, his replacement was an older minister, Mr Bury, who had previously served as a missionary in East Pakistan[62]. Mr Bury was a bachelor who lived with his spinster sister. Both men were very different but had one thing in common, which was neither of them had a preaching style that would call for fire and brimstone, far from it. While all this was going on, another Baptist minister was proving more controversial. Martin Luther King Jr. was at the time an activist and the main spearhead of the Civil Rights Movement in America. Articulating the hopes of all African Americans, liberals and right-minded observers, King also drew intense hostility, unrest, opposition, and death threats before finally being assassinated in 1968. His last sermon

---

62 An area of Pakistan that was established in 1955 and lasted until 1971 when it became Bangladesh.

referenced the story of Rip van Winkle, who slept through the American Civil War. The storybook character had missed the moment. Was America missing theirs? King's assassin was a convicted burglar who claimed his motive for the killing was so that his name could be remembered by history. For obvious reasons I am not going to dignify his action by giving his name here.

Mom and Dad integrated themselves into the fabric of the place and became church members. The church supported the relief and development charity Christian Aid, and for years Mom collected donations going door to door to collect coin-filled envelopes. She also helped with Sunday school from time to time. Dad took on the role of secretary for the Boys Brigade.

At this time, old newspapers were used as insulation for food bought in fish shops. There was a saying that today's newspaper headlines are tomorrow's chip shop wrappings. The church however had discovered a new use for unwanted newspapers. Mom enthusiastically supported this initiative. She regularly visited neighbours in the street to collect old newspapers, which the church sold as a fundraiser to a firm that supplied a cardboard manufacturer and a vehicle paint workshop. So, the old newspapers were recycled either as cardboard pulp or masking devices.

I once heard adventurer Bear Grylls being interviewed on the radio. He said he felt churches should be part hospital and part wedding. I know what he meant about weddings. There was the preparation (for key church services), the ceremony (prayers and offertory), and the celebration (church socials, fetess, day trips out and get-togethers).

Well-attended Sunday morning services were boosted even further by key events such as the children's anniversary, the nativity service, Sunday school prize giving and the Christmas carol service. Eventually the congregation outgrew the church building, and a larger structure was built on the same site, along with a manse for the minister and his family. Many of the men gave up their spare time to function as labourers in this new venture, keeping costs down.

We eventually moved from the estate and the church, and Sundays themselves changed with Sunday trading laws being removed. The restrictions that we lived under then seem unduly excessive and serve as a curious reminder of a long-bygone age. I am grateful for the lack of legalism and the freedom I enjoy today. Yet the Sundays I once knew were unlike every other day, and it was not all bad. Somehow, with the passage of time, the general idea of rest and making Sunday different has been lost. Then there is the community of Delves Baptist Church. I am grateful to have been part of it for a while.

# SOCIETAL TRENDS AND ATTITUDES

# Chapter Twelve

## *White heat and small steps*

There was nothing short of excitement in our household when we had a telephone installed. An overhead wire from a telegraph pole to our house announced its arrival to the outside world. Inside, a handset complete with a chunky circular rotary dial and a curly wire was tethered to a plug near the foot of the staircase in the hall. We had now bypassed the need to visit a red public phone box. The handset looked blankly at us. All we needed now was someone to call us. As we pondered the fact that a listing in next year's edition of the BT phone book might help, the phone rang. Mrs Craddock in the next street spotted the work being carried out, got our number from directory enquiries and was the first person to test this new marvel of modern technology.

Here in our own home, we had our piece of technological ingenuity. When someone did ring, Mom or Dad would pick up the receiver and answer very deliberately, 'Hello, Walsall 24997'. How times change. The digital revolution has taken hold in almost every corner of modern life, transforming communication along the way. Nowadays the domestic landline is fast being ditched because of the capability of mobile alternatives. The internet has revolutionised the way we communicate, understand, and do business. Everyday tasks, whether paying bills, getting a taxi, booking a holiday, or shopping, have been made more convenient and swifter to undertake. Yet much of my life has been lived before the internet came into popular use, a time when stories of technological breakthroughs set the imagination racing. Compulsive viewing in our household was a programme called *'Tomorrow's World'*, which featured new inventions and their potential benefits.

Sometimes it is a key phrase or expression that renders a leader's speech memorable and resonates with the audience's consciousness. In his inaugural address to the nation, President Kennedy argued that American citizens should not ask what the country could do for them, but what they could do for their country. The point was driven home. Civil Rights leader Martin Luther King Jr. had a dream and spelt it out in terms that everyone could understand. In this country, Winston Churchill is best remembered for his stirring wartime rhetoric and wordcraft. In peacetime, Churchill's health was failing, and he retired as Prime Minister a year before I was born to be succeeded by Anthony Eden. It was however the leader of the opposition who captured the national imagination in what has been called 'the white heat of technology' speech (see Chapter 6 earlier).

Opening a debate on science at the 1963 Labour Party conference, Harold Wilson delivered one of the most memorable political speeches of the century. Wilson painted a dynamic picture of technological change and its opportunities for industry and implication for the economy and society more generally. Calling for an end to restrictive practices and outdated methods, he pictured a new Britain forged in the 'white heat' of a scientific revolution. Wilson's speech inspired many and, in all probability, helped pave the way to a change of government and a fresh vision for the country. Technology had the potential to enhance life and increase national prosperity if only it was grasped. The question for the country was which party did voters trust to rise to the challenge? Wilson was youthful, intelligent, had the common touch, and crucially had his finger on the pulse of technology. On the other hand, Eden and his government seemed to be nothing short of 'old'. Government politicians appeared old-fashioned in their dress and ways and belonged to a party dominated by old fogies and Old Etonians. During a successful election campaign in 1964, Wilson was television savvy and maximised its potential for effective communication right into people's front rooms. In that respect Wilson was the prototype modern-day politician.

A political will and continuing advances in technology promised a brave new world. The country may have had one foot in the past, but its other foot was stepping into the future. This was an age of huge medical and scientific advances and the continuation of the bold venture of the National Health Service. It seemed to be a time when the impossible could be made possible. Until the sixties, what existed beyond this world was still largely unknown and unexplored. Technological advances meant that space travel was no longer the dream of for sci-fi enthusiasts and the comic book character Dan Dare. It has been said that long ago, humans believed they could travel on water, so they mustered sufficient technology to develop boats and ships. They then believed that they could ride horseless chariots, and the invention of the engine followed. Still restless for the new, they believed they could fly, and the aeroplane was invented. In the sixties they gazed at the night sky and believed they could explore the stars and reach the moon.

Aside from exploring the previously unexplored, technology was also being used to travel faster than ever before. Sir Donald Campbell proved himself to be the fastest person alive when breaking world records for both land speed and water speed in 1964. Tragedy, however struck in 1967 when Coniston Water in the Lake District became a watery grave for Sir Donald Campbell when attempting to break his own record in his speed boat Bluebird K7[63].

Everyday life however seemed to carry on as it always had. Dad earned a living as a draughtsman, which involved travelling to share a smoke-filled Birmingham office ten miles away. He spent forty hours a week using hard pencils and oversized paper, working cheek-by-jowl with colleagues all keeping the same hours. Next-door neighbour, Mr Buck, delivered coal for a living, returning home after he had completed his round and picking up a fresh dog bite each week for his trouble. Jack Skinner, next

---

63  The craft was travelling at 328mph at the time.

door but one, left home in the morning to run a struggling corner grocer shop in a poor area of Walsall. This was daily life for these three working men living next to one another in Lilac Avenue.

Social class and status were of greater significance in the fifties and sixties[64] than they are now, and the job you did helped define you. Dad was categorised as 'B Middle class' (middle management, administrative and professional) while Mr Buck was placed in the 'C2 Lower middle-class' category (semi and unskilled manual). I never met anyone in the 'A Upper Middle Class' category. In this brave new world could technology offer a vehicle to move out of the social class of a person's birth? Could the class-ridden country become a meritocracy?

The realisation of the world Wilson envisaged has grown organically over time. The evidence of achievement is easily recognisable today. Almost sixty years after the 'white heat of technology' speech, unprecedented measures were put in place to combat a Coronavirus (COVID-19) pandemic that claimed over six million lives worldwide. Unnecessary gatherings were prohibited, and those forced to leave home to go to a chemist or to buy food were advised to keep a two-metre social distance from others. Virtually every business, shop, place of education, pub, restaurant, and gatherings for worship were shut. Technology came to the rescue. For many, being at home was no barrier to work thanks to shared documents, teleconferencing and videoconferencing. Bitcoins, debit cards and credit cards were utilised to order food and goods that were delivered to the front door. Even means of religious worship were screened on *YouTube* and accessed through laptops, tablets, and mobiles. My grandchildren attempted to engage with online lessons. I was able to see my family through *Facetime*. I also took part in a weekly online

---

64 Marketers and others segmenting the population still use these categories to help understand socioeconomic factors.

pub quiz with friends. Such goings-on would have been well beyond the comprehension of the three men mentioned earlier.

Mr Buck would have marvelled at a system that involved online ordering, tracking deliveries, and offering payment services. Mr Skinner was already running something akin to an online shopping experience from his traditional grocery shop minus the digital element. Shopping lists would be passed to him. He would pack the order during the day, drop boxes of groceries off and collect money on the way home. All that was missing was the technology to broaden his customer base and speed up the process. Then there was Dad. Being told of computer-aided design software would have left him incredulous. Thanks to his earlier military service overseas, his courtship involved being physically separated from Mom. They compensated with regular contact through letters and photographs that were posted daily. It is a  small leap to the more modern concept of online dating, the difference being that interactions now are instant and enhanced by video.

Adults living in this specific sliver of the twentieth century could never even dream of the range and power of technology that would be at the disposal of ordinary people during the lifetime of their children. The technology that was available in the sixties was in the hands of governments and large organisations rather than individuals. The potential for using technology to enable space travel was on the agenda of the two great superpowers of the period. The Space Race was underway, and initially it looked as if the Soviets were in the ascendancy. My brother was exactly two years old on 12 April 1961 when Yuri Gagarin became the first human to journey into outer space. Completing one orbit of the earth in his capsule, Vostok 1, he returned safely to report, *'I looked and looked, but I didn't see God'*. To borrow a phrase from the science fiction television programme of the period *Star Trek* 'space the final frontier' had been conquered.

US President Kennedy upped the stakes and articulated a clear challenge – put a man (sic) on the moon before the end of the current decade. It was a target for not only his country but for his enemies also. Who would win the race? The vast financial outlays going into the Space Race began to show some notable results. In March 1965, Russian Air Force major general and Soviet cosmonaut Alexei Arkhipovich Leonov became the first person to spacewalk (for a full twelve minutes and nine seconds). Lauded as a hero back in the Soviet Union, he was selected to be the first cosmonaut to set foot on the moon. In the event the project was cancelled, and it was left to an American astronaut[65], Neil Armstrong, to complete the task just four years later.

So it was that, ahead of schedule on 20 July 1969, Neil Armstrong famously stepped down from the Apollo 11 Lunar Module Eagle onto the moon's surface. Kennedy himself never lived to see the event being cruelly gunned down by an assassin's bullet many years earlier. He missed hearing Armstrong's well-rehearsed but ultimately fluffed line of *'That's one small step for man, one giant leap for mankind.'* (He should have said 'a man'). A modern rendering of this well-remembered soundbite would surely be nearer: *'That's one small step for a human, one giant leap for humankind'.*

It has been estimated that a single modern mobile phone has got several million times more memory and 100,000 times more processing power than the Americans had at their disposal to get men to the moon. This underlines both the determination of those responsible for the Apollo programme and the fact that technological advances march ever onwards.

---

65  I discovered quite recently that a translation of the word astronaut means star sailor, and this seems entirely appropriate as they continued a tradition that was evident in sailors who sought new continents and circumnavigated the earth by ship.

By the time of the landing, my family had relocated from Yew Tree estate, and I had hit my teens. I suppose I should recall the televised moon landing vividly. The BBC always finished broadcasts at twelve midnight by playing the national anthem. If the TV set was left on after this point, viewers would encounter a white dot on the screen and a long buzzing noise. The moon landing was different, the magnitude of the occasion meant that the BBC broadcast the event continuously throughout the night. Up to 650 million people worldwide, including twenty-two million Britons, tuned in to see the moon landing. This may have been the biggest TV audience ever, but I cannot truthfully tell interesting anecdotes about it. I was in bed. I suppose I was not interested enough in the moon landing to miss a night's sleep[66].

I may not have seen a minute of the drama unfolding, but I obviously remember the immediate aftermath. Front pages of the newspapers carried the images for days on end. Like everyone else, I heard 'One small step …' repeated many times on radio and television and saw grainy black and white replays of the space pioneers Neil Armstrong and 'Buzz Aldrin' dancing like embarrassing dads at a gravity-less family party. The astronauts had proved that humans could survive stepping onto another planet. They scooped up surface and rock samples and to underline their country's supremacy over the Soviets, planted the stars and stripes flag of the United States into the dusty planet's surface.

All newspapers carried special editions, some with wraparound front colour pages. The most striking thing for me after seeing these pictures was not the power of the space craft, the sense of achievement, or the bravery of the astronauts. It was instead the object in the background of one of the pictures. The object in question was an inviting blue sphere over the moon pioneer's shoulder. The contrast between the appearance of

---

66 I take some comfort from the fact that thirty-four million Britons were in the same boat!

the vibrant, enchanting earth and the dead, grey moon could not have been greater. If the culmination of the Space Race and 240,000 miles travel taught me something it was a recognition that I am blessed to live on a beautiful planet. To counter Yuri Gagarin's failure to see God eight years earlier, Aldrin read from John's Gospel and performed a communion service. I am not sure what specific verses Aldrin read but the best-known verse in the New Testament is to be found in John 3:16[67]. The natural reaction is to concentrate on the part of the verse that explains what must be done to inherit eternal life. This overlooks the first part of the sentence that God loves the world. No wonder He does. Little wonder too that reform leader John Calvin described the earth as the theatre of God's glory. Here, suspended in the blackness of space, was a thing of beauty, and all humankind had to do was take good care of it.

The Space Race was a spectacular adventure that lasted for the best part of two decades. As part of an ongoing Cold War, achievements from the programme offered propaganda opportunities for both sides. More practically the Race was also a good proxy for a real war, and thousands enjoyed employment working on different projects. Then there are the spin-off benefits that have since had a wider application, including fire detectors, cordless power tools, satellite television and cellular phones. Even more impressively the internet came about building on the protocols and architecture developed[68] to share work collaboratively. The technological advances and the American 'can do' approach were undeniable and admirable. I am, however, left feeling uncomfortable about it all.

---

67 'For God so loved the world that he gave his one and only Son, that whoever believes in him shall not perish but have eternal life.'

68 Vinton Cerf and Robert Kahn are credited with building on the way technology was designed to help scientists and engineers in different locations share work and double check results.

I have a CD in my collection that contains the complete collection of legendary blues singer/songwriter Robert Johnson. A significant influence on later rock superstars[69], Johnson was a true pioneer. On the inside cover of the CD are some photographs of the great man. One picture features Johnson taking a drink from a water butt marked 'coloureds only'. Either side of the butt are signs for the WCs separating white women from coloured women and white men from coloured men. Johnson makes no political point, he just stands there drinking water in a culture of division and prejudice. He quietly inhabits the only world he knows or understands. To modern eyes the sight is repellent.

The billions of dollars spent and the effort and spirit driving the Space Race could have been directed instead on less spectacular but vital areas of American life. The American Civil Rights Movement drove the passing of landmark legislation in areas such as human rights, voting and housing. The country of this period was however very firmly a dual society based on skin colour, a nation deliberately separated and unequal. Then there is the involvement of the Soviets. There was a huge redirection of national wealth into the Space Race while large swathes of its citizens lived in poverty. Many continued to just about survive in peasant communities while the benefits of modern living passed them by. The Space Race was not cost neutral[70], with many alternative national priorities ignored and opportunities forgone.

Modern information technology generally seems to have hijacked the language that meant something entirely different when I was growing up. For instance, a cursor was someone who swore, logging on was for lumberjacks, the mouse was an unwelcome visitor to the home, and a laptop was the end of the area

---

69 Eric Clapton, Bob Dylan, Robert Plant, and the Rolling Stones all have cited Johnson as an influence.

70 Estimates vary but are costs are thought to be more than $25 billion for the United States.

that you sat on when on a mother's knee. Perhaps job titles are the clearest indicators of the change that has happened over time. Growing up people had jobs such as chargehands, foremen, bus conductors, work study officers, comptometer operators, and typists[71]. Virtually all these roles have disappeared or have been absorbed into newer ones. Now jobs are advertised reflecting a new world where analytics and data services are important. My childhood pre-dates by twenty-odd years what has since been called the digital revolution. The technology that operated in the world I grew up in was more mechanical and manually dependent. A rapid pace of change driven by developments and improvements in communications, computers and the introduction of the internet only occurred towards the end of my working life[72]. The white heat of technology continues to glow brightly today, driving change as it does so.

71 Chargehands and the higher-ranking foremen were responsible for the work of others in a factory setting. Bus conductors' sole job was to collect fares on public transport. Work study officers aimed to improve efficiency of working practices through measurement and observation. Comptometer operators performed calculations on a key-driven mechanical machine, and it was the specialist job of typists to convert handwritten documents into print through a typewriter often operating in a typing pool.

72 Today a further revolution is underway with technologies such as cloud computing, big data, data analytics, process automation, artificial intelligence, data visualisation, blockchain, internet of things, mobile technologies, and 3-D printing.

# Chapter Thirteen

## *It's complicated*

The year before Mom and Dad got married, they had a day out in London. Travelling by train to see 'The Festival of Britain', the journey doubtless involved seeing a landscape still scarred by war with bombed out buildings and craters. At the time rationing persisted and the green shoots of national recovery still seemed very delicate, so the celebration was a welcome and a well-deserved fillip for the whole nation. The feel-good occasion was organised to mark the centenary of the Great Exhibition of 1851[73] but drew the scorn of the leader of the opposition, Winston Churchill, who grumpily decried it as a piece of socialist propaganda and a cheap stunt to gain votes in the upcoming general election[74]. Despite Churchill's comments the event proved a huge commercial and popular success and ran for five months, attracting eight million visitors along the way (two million more than the Great Exhibition). A significant difference in emphasis of this later event was that this time it was not a world fair, it was exclusively and unashamedly British. Even the Commonwealth did not get a look in. It was an event celebrating and promoting all that is good in Britain, including science

---

73  The Great Exhibition of 1851 was held in Hyde Park, London inside a vast purpose-built structure of iron and glass known as the Crystal Palace. Most of the cast iron used was produced in the Black Country. The prototype trade show was hugely popular with examples of the best of Victorian invention and technology as well as displays of objects from around the world.

74  In the event Labour polled almost a quarter of a million votes more than their opponents but due to the quirkiness of our 'first past the post' voting system a new Conservative government was elected with a majority of seventeen seats.

and technology, industry, architecture, and the arts. The event highlighted Great Britain with the emphasis on 'great'.

Nowadays, online forms make the task of national self-identification straightforward by limiting the options. For instance, there is often a pulldown box to aid in answering the question 'what nationality are you?' The option of 'UK' in the listing saves the dilemma of deciding whether I am English or British. When I was growing up Scotland eroded my feeling of Britishness. This mighty area dominating the north of the British Isles seemed to be so different geographically that it was difficult to believe I inhabited the same country. Apart from the unique landscape, Scotland had their own bank notes. Dad somehow once ended up with a Scottish pound note, which contained a picturesque and elaborate design issued by the Bank of Clydeside (or somewhere similar). It did however have one major disadvantage. None of the local shopkeepers would accept it. The difficulty was only resolved when Mom visited the Co-op bank in Walsall town centre and exchanged it for a 'real' pound note at the counter. The differences did not stop there, there was Scotland's unique customs and dress and, unlike the rest of the country, Scotland did not celebrate Christmas as a bank holiday.

The Scots may have failed to recognise Christmas, but they did provide the rest of the nation with a televised Hogmanay event. As New Year's Eve came around, we had nothing better to do than watch the programme. What was special was a later bedtime and the possibility of a small glass of the custard-type treat of *Warninks Advocaat*. Other Christmas leftovers, such as mince pies and shortbread biscuits were also in evidence as our family settled down to watch the tame spectacle of *Andy Stewart's White Heather Club*. Santa only made an appearance around Christmastime, and Stewart seemingly was only in evidence one night of the year, and this was it. The kilted star of the show sang jolly folk songs with strange words while simultaneously smiling and winking at the camera. He was joined by nimble-footed female dancers who negotiated crossed swords and wore tartan dresses. Our artificial silver Christmas tree that had long lost its sparkle surveyed the scene with apparent boredom.

I liked porridge, shortbread, and oat cakes, but if Hogmanay goings on like this was part of Britishness, then I was not British. Men clutching bagpipes and wearing tartan kilts was something completely alien[75]. The packet of *Scotts Porridge Oats* in the cupboard, which depicted a muscular kilted man engaging in a highland games event, was quite unlike anything I had ever witnessed, even in the Walsall Arboretum. I suppose I felt English by default, even though I did not know of anyone who looked like the sailor on the boxes of *England's Glory* matches. The patriotism I felt when England won the World Cup in 1966 was undeniable. Even at the scene of England's greatest sporting triumph there was a conflicted crowd as the waving flags were not the white and red cross of St. George, but red, white, and blue flags of the union. No wonder there was confusion, unlike Wales and Scotland, England does not have a national anthem it can call its own. Instead, it shares a British anthem that celebrates the monarch rather than the country. Then there was the cartoon character John Bull, was he meant to be British or English? These thoughts left me nowhere nearer deciding if I was British or English.

I may have been conflicted on this issue, but the thought of being European did not exercise my mind at all at that time. John Donne's much-quoted phrase about not being an island[76]

---

75 Of course, this was grossly unfair of me. It was like thinking that Wales was jam packed with women in tall chimney hats, wearing shawls and carrying harps. Or for that matter that London was populated by people dressed either as beefeaters, bowler hatted businessmen or pearly kings and queens.

76 John Donne's 1624 poem uses the phrase 'no man is an island'.

underlines the human yearning for connection to others and the need for community. Virtually every society would find some resonance in the sentiments of this poet and scholar from four hundred years ago. For Britain of the fifties and sixties, however, the thinking might have been along the lines of 'yes, but it's complicated'. This archipelago's physical separation from Europe served it well a few years earlier during the Second World War. Now there was an opportunity to form an economic European partnership and forge trading ties with near neighbours. However, Britain's eccentricities and 'the way things are done around here' functioned as a shield to foreign influence and a potential barrier to such cooperation. Maybe integration beyond keeping a bottle of Dutch advocaat in the house every Christmas was a step too far for the nation?

Following talks involving Belgium, France, Italy, Luxembourg, the Netherlands, and West Germany, the Treaty of Rome was signed in March 1957. The resultant European Economic Community (EEC) was born on 1 January 1958. Seeking to work towards cooperation and economic growth through trade, the community established a common market based on the free movement of goods, people, services, and capital. The belief was that closer union would not only bring economic benefits but crucially would lessen the chance of armed conflict between these near neighbours in the future. After being initially keen on the idea the British government declined to be fully involved in talks and so missed out.

Opponents of entry into the EEC made claims of trade opportunities elsewhere, possibly in Commonwealth countries. With decolonisation, self-governance and independence, former dominions, colonies and the like now represented a Commonwealth sustained by voluntary association. The Commonwealth offered a distant reminder of a British Empire of many varied countries spread across the globe and ruled from London. These were territories acquired through settlement or conquest and represented a source of national pride and wealth. The Empire began breaking up soon after the turn of the twentieth century, but despite this my junior school still told us stories of the achievement of white men on its behalf. Legacies of the Empire were still apparent in everyday items. Metal objects in both the cutlery drawer and Dad's tool kit were stamped with the words 'Empire made'. Then there was the *Camp coffee* on my grandparent's kitchen shelf. This ultra-sweet syrupy coffee and chicory concentrate was in liquid form and came in a bottle complete with an evocative label. Conjuring a vision of a golden era sometime in the past in a faraway land, it featured a white moustachioed officer, resplendent in a kilt taking time out from running the Empire to drink a leisurely cuppa. An Asian man took on the role of servant and was pictured hovering in the background, waiting for his master to finish[77].

Today the Commonwealth continues but represents only nine per cent of this country's trade. Meanwhile the EEC has morphed into the EU, involves many more countries, and represents the largest trading bloc in the world. Recently the UK has extracted itself from the union after forty-odd years membership. How different this was to the sixties, when the emphasis was upon trying to gain a belated entry. Such efforts were rebuffed by the veto of the French and, in particular, the opposition of their President, Charles de Gaulle.

When de Gaulle listed several aspects of Britain's economy and working practices, which made our country incompatible with Europe, he had a point[78]. Initial hesitancy and a lack of early engagement could be interpreted as the British wanting to be different. The country appeared to have set out to make it, if not impossible, then extremely difficult to integrate with mainland

---

77  More recently the brand image has been softened so that the servant joins the officer for a drink.

78  Only after much debate, deliberation, negotiation, and a referendum (not to mention de Gaulle's death) did Britain finally assume membership of the community much later in 1973.

Europe, not least because of a failure to recognise decimals! The great British public bought cheese by the ounce, potatoes by the pound and petrol by the gallon. They drank beer, bought milk, and gave blood by the pint. Measurement was in feet and inches so that a school sports day involved the 100-yard dash rather than the one hundred metres event their continental counterparts experienced. The British version would, of course, probably result in a quicker finish, not through superior athleticism but because there was a mere 91.44 metres to cover. Even today, all these years later, I find it impossible to think of volumes, sizes, and distances in any way other.

Our currency had served the country well since Anglo Saxon times. The system involved pounds, shillings, and pence; there were twelve pence to a shilling and twenty shillings to a pound[79]. Foreigners attempting to get to grips with this strange monetary system, may trip over the complication of guineas[80]. To make the currency even more impenetrable, coins themselves had nicknames, for instance a bob (a shilling), a half crown (two shillings and sixpence), a florin (two shillings) and a tanner (sixpence).

Britain's distinctiveness extends far beyond measurement and currency. Britons drive on the left-hand side of the road, a distinction shared with Nepal and Cyprus[81]. Do we believe that the rest of the right-hand side driving world are out of line? Even

---

79 Pounds, shillings, and pence were represented by the symbols £, s, d. Just as the date is represented by numbers separated by a backslash symbol so the price of something for 11 pounds, 10 shillings and sixpence would be shown as £11/10s/6d. The pence symbol d was borrowed from the Roman denarii, a legacy of an ancient coin used by an invading people.

80 One pound, one shilling since you ask. The currency was only decimalised in 1971 but guineas still persist in horse racing as prize money.

81 Some former British colonies also drove on the left-hand side of the road.

as late as the seventies we had our own slightly bigger version of A4 paper, known as foolscap, which resulted in the production of different-sized office paperwork and files for the home market. Then there is the matter of shoe size. While British men walked about in size nine shoes, their European counterparts with the same sized feet wore shoes of 39-40 (and doubtlessly inferior footwear too). Furthermore, we boasted different sized spanners nuts and bolts, which required imperial spanners. In these days before digital time pieces, everyone wore analogue winding watches. The twenty-four-hour clock was rarely used, with Britain's preferring to use the more homely twelve hour am (ante meridiem, before noon) and pm (post meridiem after noon) system. The twenty-four-hour clock seemed too continental by half. So, it went on. When Donne wrote, *'every man is a piece of the continent, a part of the main. If a clod be washed away by the sea, Europe is the less'* he had not taken these points into account. This British clod had its own way of doing things. If anything, cultural reference points and societal influences seemed to come more from the other side of the Atlantic than the twenty miles across the English Channel in continental Europe.

By the mid-sixties, patriotism and long-established social norms were under threat. The uprising took shape most prominently on America's west coast. Part way through 1967, in a neighbourhood of San Francisco, something very strange happened. An eclectic group of 100,000 young people, some in distinctive hippie dress, joined together to engage in what mattered to them in a summer of love. This involved hippie and acid rock music, drug taking, anti-Viet Nam war protests, and free love. Clearly this was a direct challenge to the establishment of the day. The British got a sanitised version of the uprising the following year. Our media latched onto phrases like 'flower power', 'the summer of love', and the command 'to make love not war'. Meanwhile, corporations saw the commercial possibilities and a market for items such as tie-dye tea shirts, kaftans, and beads. Psychedelic designs were soon in evidence on clothing, wallpaper, soft furnishings, and posters on the wall.

The more radical aspects of the summer of love, however, hardly pricked the surface of the Yew Tree estate subculture. Residents continued to live their neat semi-detached lives, engaging in respectable routines of cooking Sunday roasts, mowing the lawn, and putting the bins out every Wednesday morning. Ordinary blokes went to ordinary jobs at the same time and came home at the same time, all returning to ordinary homes, wives, kids, and evening meals. Women apparently accepted the loss of career opportunities and freedoms in return for raising a family. Having lived through the hardship and horror of a world war to experience this mundane stability must have seemed infinitely preferable.

This was a time when couples living together were always married to one another. For the main part households on the estate conformed to the definition of a nuclear family, containing a family group of two biological parents and their offspring. The parents had, in all probability, grown up in an extended family home, and they were glad to be rid of it. This was different, this was Yew Tree estate. Grandparents were separately housed somewhere off the estate. I did not know of any single-parent families or stepchildren. Blending was for instant coffee and whisky, not families. This was a community where women worked until they had children at a time long before maternity leave[82] and other rights were introduced. Mothers became housewives as it was termed then[83], while their husbands continued to work. In the absence of paternity leave, men could mark the birth of their offspring by carrying on working, booking annual leave, or losing pay to stay home for a few days.

On a visit to Walsall market, I once overheard a conversation where one man was described as a good husband because he

---

82 Maternity leave was not introduced until 1975, and paternity leave not until 2003.

83 Home maker is a less gendered more modern term.

worked hard all week and handed over his pay packet on Fridays. His wife returned pocket money for a pint or two down the pub. Norms for what constituted a good partner clearly differed then from now. Being a good companion, being kind and loving, caring for the children and sharing a life clearly had second billing to working hard, handing over your money, and not messing with other women. The deal was that women did the childcare, cleaning, cooking, and housekeeping. Men earned the money, maintained cars, kept the garden tidy and did DIY.

This household rhythm is very gendered by modern standards but seemed 'normal' at the time. While women earned the tag of housewives, men were often referred to by enquiring tradespeople as the 'head of the household'. The phrase implies that one person, the man, made all the meaningful decisions, financially and otherwise, on behalf of the household. Our own domestic arrangements broke this stereotype. Mom had a tight grip on the family budget and Dad went along with her assessment of what we could and could not afford as a family[84].

The LGBTQ+ agenda rightly commands attention today. Back then such matters were never discussed, and closet doors remained firmly closed. I only ever encountered two lesbian couples, both at church, and no gay couples. I was unfamiliar with the word 'lesbian' or indeed 'homosexual' or any other word or term of this nature. (If a word containing 'sexual' was used within earshot, it would have earned a rebuke from Mom anyway.) Being gay was universally understood as being joyful. I was oblivious to there being an issue and, like many, believed gender to be straightforwardly binary rather than fluid or graduated. If the acronym LGBTQ+ had been about at this time, then it would have been taken for being the title of one of the powerful trade union groups[85].

---

84 Mom always erred on the side of caution in these matters.
85 Possibly the Local Government Boilermakers and Transport union?

This was the world in which I grew up. At one level matters seemed very uncomplicated. Unfortunately, such thinking ignored a complexity of issues, including sexist stereotyping, inequality, minority rights and the possible xenophobia shaping our relationship with other European nations. Then of course there is the legacy of colonisation. Empire labelled oddments about the house and labels on coffee jars are artefacts of a darker story. Western civilisation benefitted economically, culturally, and socially from colonialism. Britain's past is far from happy and glorious when the sordid and inhumane slave trade is considered. The capture, trade, and exploitation of Africans as slave labour on Caribbean and American sugar and cotton plantations was hugely profitable. Men, women, and children were branded like cattle and transported in appalling overcrowded conditions. For those surviving dehydration, dysentery, and scurvy (twenty per cent did not), a life of hard labour and poverty waited for them. Founder of Methodism, John Wesley's last known letter urged the abolition of the 'execrable villainy' of the trade[86]. The country gained from the exploitation of others and, thanks to inherited wealth, continues to do so today.

Defeat in the Second World War forced both Japan and Germany to reflect, acknowledge and repent of their imperial past. For Britain such a process has been absent, meaning that questions remain even today. What form should acknowledgement take? How might repentance be achieved? What might compensation look like? Even now our nation has failed to fully face up to the pain and suffering of the victims of the trade. In

---

86 The Slave Trade Act of 1807 prohibited the slave trade operating in the British Empire. The Slavery Abolition Act of 1833 outlawed slavery itself in most parts of the Empire. This was only achieved by paying high levels of slave compensation (forty per cent of the country's yearly income) not to freed slaves to redress the injustices they suffered but to slave owners for their 'loss of property'. No reparation payment to the enslaved and their descends or apology has ever been issued.

2020, the capture on a mobile video of the murder of the black American George Floyd by white police officers was a pivotal force behind the Black Lives Matter (BLM) movement in both the USA and the UK. Protesters pointed to the objectionable presence of monuments of figures connected with slavery, and the statue of Edward Colston was toppled and dumped in Bristol harbour. The truth is any number of statues across the country could have been targeted for the same reason[87]. Perhaps 2020 marked the beginning of a shared reflection on past atrocities and present-day inequalities and racism, whether deliberate or benign and unintentional. It is a long way from perfect, but parts of today's society are becoming more sensitive to these matters. The sixties worldview dictated that there were no issues and therefore nothing needed to be addressed, but that was a lie, things were more complicated.

---

87 One of the world's most famous statues is Nelson's column, which stands 185 feet above Trafalgar Square in London. It celebrates naval hero Horatio Nelson who was a vocal opponent of William Wilberforce, the driving force behind Parliament's abolition of the slave trade.

# Chapter Fourteen

## *Never had it so good?*

Someone once observed that life is formally recorded as a dash between two dates. I was born a healthy eight-pound twelve-ounce addition to my family, the start of a new generation and the lowest branch of a family tree. My first date of 1956 was now in place. Sixty-odd years later, I have involuntarily moved to the highest branch on the family tree with two generations below me and find myself closer to my second date than my first. Most of the adults I knew as a child have now acquired a full set of dates and a dash. Along the way, my life has straddled the vastly different worlds of then and now. My body feels frailer than it once did, but I seem to have acquired a sharpened memory of the then, the incidents in my early life. I suppose some early memories involve a combination of things half remembered and half forgotten. Other memories are crystal clear, as if they happened yesterday. Memories like a pre-school version of myself lying awake at night studying the wallpaper in my room.

The curtains in my bedroom let in light. The warm wind from the partly opened window gently billowed the curtains in soothing waves against the windowsill edge. I could hear the muffled sound of Mom and Dad talking downstairs and the odd sound from the street. The room still had the scent of fresh white gloss paint and wallpaper glue which suppressed any smell there might be from the sewerage works. As I lay there my eyes surveyed the newly papered walls. Images of Enid Blyton's story book character *Noddy* and his friends now dominated the room. Where the edges of wallpaper met, there was a slight mismatch making it look as if *Big Ears'* bicycle had been badly welded together from two separate bikes. Worse, *PC Plod's* arm looked as if it had been severed off and re-attached in a cavalier fashion[88]. A room specially decorated just for me; I was fortunate indeed.

My then life was an ordinary one, but one played out in extraordinary times. The world of then was a particular time in history and of place that looks strange from the vantage point of now. Despite the demands for change, then still clung to the past with its traditions, legacies, and old school values like a fading comfort blanket. The past reeked of a pre-war Britain, a former Empire, a well-established class system and 'knowing your place'. Firmly established archaic institutions like the monarchy and an unelected upper parliamentary chamber[89] reinforced the differences in class and the lack of opportunity in society. The message was clear – some were born to rule, others, like us, were not. No change there. The then people I knew had a strong work ethic born out of a Black Country heritage, a respect for authority and possessed a moral code that demanded they live 'respectable' lives, whatever that meant.

As the nineteen fifties gave way to the sixties, society was mired in the past. The death penalty still applied[90] and other old legacies persisted, none quirkier than a daily rum ration given to sailors on Royal Navy ships. More seriously, irrational bias and personal prejudice was given full legal licence. In the workplace it was possible to hire or fire an employee and apply different pay rates based upon their

---

88 *Noddy* and *Big Ears* also found their way into our kitchen in the form of two egg cups that contained space for boiled eggs in the place where their hats should have been.

89 The very name of the upper chamber, the House of Lords, confirmed as much to us, the commoners!

90 The Murder (Abolition of Death Penalty) Act 1965 led to suspension of the penalty before it was permanently outlawed in 1969.

gender[91]. Someone could be prevented from entering a pub or refused accommodation simply because they did not have the right skin colour. It was also a dangerous time to be gay – homosexual activity was punishable by imprisonment after all. Despite all this, the then world knew that change was on the agenda, and there was a general desire for a brighter more affluent future.

With the economy in mind, a Prime Minister of the period, Harold Macmillan ('Supermac'), lectured us that we had 'never had it so good'. It is true that post-war Britain was at last starting to shape up. The policies intended to get the country back on its feet after the war had continued under successive governments and were now starting to pay off. Both major parties shared a commitment to achieving full employment and funding a welfare state. Despite initial misgivings by some, the NHS was also proving its worth. One in three of the country's (predominantly male) workforce was now employed in manufacturing. Even if management was sometimes amateurish and there were industrial relations problems, companies were profitable. Increased steel, motor car and coal production resulted in significant economic growth, bringing with it increased disposable income and a general raising of the standard of living. The chronic shortage of housing was being tackled and rationing and national service were being shaken off. Immediate post-war austerity was giving way to modernity and there was some evidence of consumerism.

With Mom leaving work to care for two pre-school children, Dad was the sole wage earner. He enjoyed the security of a steady income, union protection and good promotion prospects. The

---

91 The Equal Pay Act of 1963 sought to ensure that women are paid equally to men in the same job. The Civil Rights Act of 1964 further established equality in the workplace, outlawing hiring and firing based on gender.

four of us represented a modern independent family unit. Mom and Dad's forebears had endured far less favourable working conditions, and once married, a lack of income forced them to share multi-generation homes. 26 Lilac Avenue was a new build when Mom and Dad took possession of it. The features of a new house that are taken for granted today, like insulation, sound proofing, central heating and double glazing, were absent. However, this was a brand-new modern structure, a fresh start and an undeniable 'step up' in the world.

The benefits of the internet and the collection of electronic gadgets that are all too apparent in today's homes were obviously absent, but things were improving. In terms of household possessions, our home boasted a television set, a fridge (with a modest freezer tray compartment), a standalone cooker, a pinewood effect radiogram with a built-in record player that resembled a piece of sideboard furniture and a Hotpoint twin tub washer. The washer featured two separate top-loading sections, one for washing and one for spin-drying wet washing. The machine frequently dripped water on the linoleum floored kitchen and shook violently. It did however make the Monday morning washing chore much easier. All these things, leaky washer included, were a positive step-change from what had gone on before. Nan and Grandad's generation and social class never dared to dream of owning a car or their own house when they were young, let alone a house full of devices and possessions that saved time and offered entertainment and comfort.

Electricity, as a universal domestic energy source, was relatively new and was being used in different ways in homes such as ours. Mom dried her hair in rollers sitting underneath an electrical contraption that blew heated air through a tube into an inflatable bonnet. Dad dispensed with his safety razor, shaving cream and brush that had served him so well in the forces in favour of an electric razor. Artificially illuminated coals or logs on electric fires were fooling no one that they might be real; they did however make their statement – this is effective, easy, and new. This is now.

The psychedelic movement was an influence on design and colours in the home, and statement furniture and decoration were a welcome break from the gloomy decade of rationing. We had very 'of the period' yellow Formica tops on work surfaces in the kitchen and curtains in the lounge with large gaudy swirling patterns. Mom described designs such as these as 'bobby dazzlers' or 'humdingers' or 'jazzy'.

New materials were beginning to dominate modern 1960s family homes. Clothes shoppers were no longer restricted to natural fabrics like wool and cotton. Contemporary chipboard wardrobes across the estate now contained competitively priced clothes made of fabrics first developed in science labs. Nylon, polythene, and other plastics that originally had wartime uses now found a new market, the consumer market. Dad had several off-the-peg suits made of or including synthetic material, a vast number of nylon shirts and numerous polyester ties in distinctive colours and patterns. The chemical conglomerate Imperial Chemical Industries (ICI) was a British success story of the period. Along with manufacturing general chemicals, paints, pharmaceuticals, fragrances and food flavourings, the company became the unlikely source of a very sixties trend for modern women's fashions such as crimplene or terylene dresses and suits.

The use of Bakelite, a form of moulded plastic with heat-resistant, non-electrically conductive properties, was also very much in evidence in the home in the form of electric switches, plugs and radio sets. In the kitchen it was also an ideal material for saucepan handles. At the end of his working life, Dad's father Job worked at the large engineering company J.A. Crabtree in Walsall producing Bakelite electrical components. Bakelite was eventually replaced by other durable, heat resistant and potentially more colourful plastics. Materials like wood, pottery and tin may have dominated their parents' kitchens, but for the modern family the accent was on the new. Plastic's versatility meant it could be shaped into rigid but lightweight containers of all shapes and sizes, the most well-known range being branded as 'Tupperware'. The company's 'revolutionary' containers were inexpensive to produce, a darling of American housewives in the fifties, and for sixties British families the next 'new thing'. Tupperware operated a successful business model based on small scale parties held in people's homes. Supposedly, a practical demonstration of how the containers could be properly closed to become airtight, the company used parties as a low-cost way of shortening the supply chain. Housewives become agents, threw parties, and invited their friends to view and then buy indispensable preparation, storage, and serving products for the kitchen and home. Partygoers put up with the pressure to buy something in return for a harmless get together while their husbands, for once, stayed at home and put the kids to bed. Mom went to a few parties, and within a week or so of the event our house was restocked with the must-have containers.

American influence was everywhere. During the forties, US soldiers stationed in this country brought with them novelties that acted as gifts for locals, like nylon stockings for women and chewing gum and comics for children. By the 1950s, aspects of American culture and consumerism were finding their way into British life, helped by imported American television programmes and films. Some direct imports of American life took place, such as Tupperware and stockings (which later evolved into tights), while others were anglicised for the British market.

Today it is suggested that the UK spends over £7 billion a year on fast food and take away burgers and chicken. McDonald's, as a market leader, has more than 1,200 restaurants in the UK alone. Things were very different in the early sixties. The country's first fast food restaurant first appeared in 1954. The British public were familiar with the American cartoon character Popeye, and one of his friends by the name of Wimpy always seemed to be munching hamburgers. So it was that Britain's first venture in this area was a Wimpy bar. The restaurant blazed a trail adapted to British sensitivities. It came complete with tablecloths, waitress service, and a menu board that incorporated pots of tea, ham, and sardine rolls alongside the fries, burgers, and milkshakes. Chewing gum was also on sale when I was a child, but again it was not a direct import. It took the form of sweet, white-coated tablets of *Beechnut* gum, which could be dispensed from a slot machine outside newspaper shops. The bonus of getting a pack free every fourth turn encouraged children to part with a penny coin for the privilege.

Nowadays it is possible to make a swift visit to a choice of supermarkets, self-select an item or two and then pay by card at a quick serve or self-serve till. Such behaviour would have been completely alien to a shopper of this earlier period. In the early sixties, the Americans had their super stores, but for many British shoppers this was a step too far. Britons had grown used to queuing for food while rationing was on, so the comfortingly long-winded and labour-intensive process continued, allowing for plenty of gossip and catching up. Once at the head of a queue, requests were made of a grocer from a pre-prepared shopping list. The shop would be assembled in a spare cardboard box or in the shopper's bag. Some brown paper bags might also be used along the way. The bill would be calculated, often mentally, by the shop assistant and settled from the cash carried in purses and wallets. Most grocery stores, if not run by the Co-op, were operated by small independent traders. Supermarkets seemed very American and lacked the personal touch that British shoppers had grown accustomed to.

Motor fuel sales in those days followed a similar theme and involved the use of petrol pump attendants. Customers never moved far from their cars when refuelling took place. Instead, they were required to engage in chit-chat with the pump attendant. Once the vehicle was filled with one of the choices available, of either two or four-star petrol, payment involved writing a paper cheque or paying cash and waiting for the change to be brought out from the kiosk before departing the pumps. A far cry from today's self-service arrangements.

These are things I recall of then. One of the problems with then was that little thought was given to environmental considerations. This was decades before the green political agenda emerged, and phrases like the 'ecosystem', 'ozone layer' or 'global warming' simply did not exist. I was unaware of any pressure groups pushing the agenda and I never heard a single person even mention environmental matters. The idea that our actions and lifestyle might be harming the planet had yet to find any place in the nation's consciousness.

In retrospect, some practices were quite environmentally friendly, while others were quite the opposite. For instance, household recycling was an unknown concept. All non-food waste went directly into a single metal dustbin that was collected weekly, loaded onto a corporation dust cart and carried away to the council dump (bad). More positively, food waste such as vegetable peelings went onto the family's compost heap in the garden, and there was much less product packaging to dispose of than there is now (good). Garden fires to get rid of waste were also a regular feature of life on the estate (bad).

Today print newspaper sales are declining and have been for many years. Back then sales were booming with the consequence that discarded papers abounded in family homes. Repurposing possibilities were legion. The traditional British version of takeaway food, fish and chips, came wrapped in old newspapers for insulation (good). Some families turned old newspapers into spills (good) to be used lighting household fires (bad), and some poorer families even cut the newspapers into squares to be used as a toilet roll substitute[92]! Mom collected old newspapers from neighbours on behalf of the church. These were sold to a company and reused (good). Some were used as part of cardboard manufacture (good), and others as masking parts of car bodies when they were resprayed (bad).

---

92 You decide whether this was good or bad!

I also remember newspapers being soaked in a bucket of wallpaper paste and moulded into papier-mâché shapes during craft lessons at school.

Virtually all bottles and liquid containers were made of glass. The return of beer bottles to off licences, and fizzy drinks bottles to shops was encouraged by offering a small monetary reward (such as three pence a bottle). A family's acquisition of milk seemed to be quite environmentally friendly. It was delivered to doorsteps using battery-powered vehicles and dispensed in glass bottles. Empty bottles were collected at the same time and returned to the depot for re-use. The bottles themselves held a pint and were simply sealed by a foil top. In some regions these tops were known to have been pierced by cheeky birds. (The absence of trees on the estate discouraged birds, so this did not present a problem for us.) Even the foil could be rescued from the rubbish dump. *Blue Peter*, the children's TV show, appealed for used tops to be posted in as part of a scheme whereby they could sell the foil on and buy a guide dog for the blind. The milk itself was so creamy that the top inch of the bottle would be a yellowish colour. The civilised thing to do was to shake the bottle before opening. The less civilised was to get to the bottle first in a morning and hog all the cream over the top of a bowl of cornflakes. On cold, snowy or frosty days, the milk had to be defrosted before it made its way into the fridge.

Then was vastly different from the world of now in many ways, not least everyday life, practices, and values. Despite all this the world of then was changing. The country's newfound optimism meant it was keen to move from austerity to modernity and embrace the new, including American cultural influences. 'Supermac' may have been right. Given what previous generations had endured the nation never had it so good as it did then.

There was a cost to this advancement, however, certainly when measured in environmental terms. Heavy industry and coal production were significant contributors to the nation's wealth, now they are seen as enemies of the climate[93]. Then there is plastic. Uncritically heralded as a wonder substance then, it is now seen as one of the planet's biggest enemies. Now plastic packaging and bags dominate the world's landfill sites, along with other manufactured materials that refuse to biodegrade easily. It has also taken on the role as the biggest polluter of the world's oceans and waterways. Once a tide recedes its presence is all too obvious on the shoreline. What is less obvious are the microscopic particles that are endangering marine life and finding their way into the human food chain. Today responsible governments are trying to reduce the production of plastic bags and other products, but the problem remains huge, serious, and difficult to tackle. The inventions, innovations, and habits of then have created a dangerous legacy for now.

Never had it so good? For some who lived through this period of history this may have been true. For the environment, minorities and the victims of hate and bias, this was far from being the case.

---

93 Now there is a broad consensus of agreement on the need to curb the rise in global warming and ensure sufficient biodiversity. Agreement on a need to sustain the planet is one thing, but nations now are either failing to take seriously or struggling to meet the carbon dioxide reduction targets they themselves set.

# Chapter Fifteen

## *The polluted goldfish bowl*

A goldfish is unaware of the environment it exists in. It never questions it, it never thinks about it, it just gets on with being a goldfish. My goldfish bowl was Yew Tree. The estate was sheltered from the influences and experiences that were more evident in nearby Walsall and West Bromwich and, indeed, other parts of the country. There were no problems with teddy boys, or the later mods and rockers, or gangs, or fights or indeed teenagers hanging about in groups. The reason was straightforward, there were very few teenagers living on the estate. There was no vandalism or graffiti to contend with. The biggest nuisance was dog mess left on grass verges. (The idea of poo bags and owners taking responsibility had yet to be articulated, let alone acknowledged.) Mom's particular difficulty, beyond cleaning up the dog mess that had been walked into the house, was contending with neighbours' garden fires on wash days. As far as anti-social behaviour went, that was it.

The community I grew up in may have been a separate goldfish bowl, but it was still a product of its time. Households for the most part reflected the standard nuclear family. This was an era when cohabitation without marriage was socially unacceptable, indeed it was referred to as 'living in sin'. Divorce was unheard of, and couples consisted of one of each gender. I cannot remember there being a single Black or Asian family living on the estate at the time. It followed that there was complete ignorance of Hindus, Muslims, Jains, Sikhs, and Buddhists and the religions they belonged to. Classes in Yew Tree Infant and Junior School comprised largely of homogeneous children of North European stock. The only children that seemed different to the rest were those from Roman Catholic homes. One such example was classmate Jill Winpenny, who lived in the house opposite in Lilac Avenue. Catholics had their multiple siblings, saints, and symbols of the crucifixion. Why was that? What was special about fish on a Friday? How is it that they are like 'us' but not like 'us'? As a child, Roman Catholics seemed interesting and exotic. Mom inadvertently added to their mystique. She had an expression for a quick wash she called a 'cat lick'. Not catching what she said properly, I thought she was saying 'catholic' very quickly. As a result, I came to believe that Catholics were people who not only expressed their Christian faith differently but also used an efficient method of personal hygiene while I wasted time taking a bath.

Given the lack of ethnic mix on the estate, diversity issues and the need for racial harmony and integration did not even register a ripple on the surface of the goldfish bowl. These matters were, however, of major significance elsewhere. Immigrants from the Commonwealth had responded to pleas to bolster a reduced labour force and help rebuild this country after the war. For those brave enough to want a new life away from Jamaica, Trinidad and Tobago and Barbados, it meant a three week plus sea journey. The irony of the crossing was surely not lost on these pioneers as they reversed the journey across the Atlantic Ocean their forebears had made in chains. Many Caribbean men had served in the armed forces during the war, now they were voluntarily responding to another plea. In doing so, men, women and whole families could make a new life for themselves in a land where there was plenty of work and hopefully a welcome. At a time when Australia operated a white-only immigration policy, it was surely logical that things would be different in Britain, particularly as some of the immigrants were war heroes?

Nearly two decades on from when the first of the 'Windrush'[94] immigrants stepped ashore, tensions were very evident just

---

94 The most significant ship carrying migrants from the Caribbean was The Empire Windrush, which left Jamaica on 24 May and arrived at Tilbury dock, Essex on 22 June 1948.

about everywhere it seemed other than on the estate. Apart from name calling and abuse, there were flashpoints of social unrest. During the summer of 1958, there were several disturbances in Notting Hill, an area in west London. Many young teddy boys were among the 400 or so white rioters that targeted individuals on the grounds of race. Colour bars also operated. At the whim of a pub and club owner not having the right colour skin could lead to exclusion. This was a truly shameful era where landlords and bed and breakfast owners could display signs making clear 'no Irish, no blacks, no dogs'. Such signs were displayed with legal impunity, drawing little if any criticism from the majority. The danger of an acquiescing or condoning culture had already been seen elsewhere. It produced a breeding ground for evil and paved the way for the atrocities committed in Stalin's Russia and by Hitler's Third Reich and many others beside.

Only six short miles away from my goldfish bowl existence, a neighbouring town earned the dubious accolade of being known as the most racist place in Britain. The local council even passed a policy to compulsorily purchase houses that came on the market in one street with the intention of letting them to white families only.

Smethwick is a typical industrial town on the southwest tip of the Black Country bordering West Bromwich. By the mid-sixties it was a place of foundries, housing shortages and a large immigrant population. The 1964 general election gave the constituency a national focus for the worst of all reasons. The campaign strategy of Conservative candidate Peter Griffiths was to exploit racial divisions to capture the working-class vote. This was a no-holds-barred approach that even involved the use of a slogan of 'if you want a n****r for a neighbour, vote Labour'.

Nationally, Labour won the election with a swing from the Tories of 3.5%. In Smethwick, a bruising campaign produced a swing in the opposite direction by a massive 7.2%. Sitting MP Patrick Walker's vote crumbled as he lost his seat to Griffiths. In the House of Commons, the new Prime Minister, Harold Wilson, called on the Tory leadership to disown Griffiths and his campaign methods. With Yorkshire bluntness he described the new MP as 'a parliamentary leper'. Twenty-five Conservatives walked out of the chamber in protest at Wilson's colourful and insulting language. On the other side of the chamber, some Labour MPs proposed a motion rebuking Wilson for insulting lepers.

Smethwick's divisions had been cruelly exploited, and these divisions had turned into gaping wounds. American civil rights and human rights activist Malcolm X was an unlikely visitor on the town's streets a year after the election. (Malcolm X was a prominent figure in the Nation of Islam and had articulated the concept of race pride.) His presence was to show solidarity with Smethwick's black and Asian minorities. He was quoted as saying:

'I am disturbed by reports that coloured people (sic) in Smethwick are being treated badly. I have heard they are being treated as the Jews were under Hitler ... I would not wait for the fascist elements in Smethwick to erect gas ovens.'

Malcolm X paid no further visits to Britain, not through a decision on his behalf, but because nine short days later he was assassinated while delivering a lecture at a ballroom in Harlem, New York.

I was blissfully ignorant of the race issue and all the shenanigans in Smethwick. I lived in a comforting environment, never observing any racist behaviour or hearing any overtly racist views expressed. Life followed a pattern unencumbered by such weighty matters, and routines like settling down with the rest of the family to watch primetime television were observed. In the early days of radio entire families would gather around wireless sets. The television set was now the shared focus. While racism may not have been explicit, the water in my bowl was being quietly polluted by insidious, covert means. The pollutant was this shared family pleasure of television. One popular prime time show that was considered the height of light entertainment was *The Black and White Minstrel Show*. I can't remember it not being part of the family's Saturday evening routine (the show had begun showing as long ago as 1958). Even though I saw the show many times, it was not really a favourite of mine. I was not fond of the corny sing-along songs and dancing, but I did enjoy the comedy routines. I do not know why, but I never questioned why the male singers and dancers wore black face makeup, had oversized white lips and wore curly wigs. I just accepted it as a familiar aspect of the show. I suppose I regarded the black face paint in the same way that I viewed white-faced Pierrot clowns, it was just one of those things they did. At some point, probably a wet and dreary Sunday afternoon, I must have caught snatches of the tedious and sentimental film The Jolson Story being shown on TV. At times during the film, Jolson was 'blacked up' following the theatrical convention started in the mid-19th century in America. It is thought that the reason for the practice was to introduce folk, jazz and blues songs to white American audiences in a palatable way through white performers who were obviously in disguise.

The popularity of *The Black and White Minstrel Show*[95] was beyond doubt with audiences peaking at around 16.5 million[96]. The possibility of offending the black community was overridden in a quest to entertain the majority white audience. In May 1967, the Campaign Against Racial Discrimination submitted a petition to the BBC calling for the show to be taken off the air. The petition was organised by Clive West, a Caribbean by birth who referred to 'this hideous impersonation' and the offence and distress caused 'to most coloured (sic) people'. The show clearly promoted and perpetuated black stereotypes while trivialising and poking fun at another culture. Eventually the show was axed, but only after a further eleven years. To say

---

95 Broadcasts involved red and white makeup being applied due to vagaries of black and white TV.
96 Obviously, the limited choice of alternative channels also played a part.

that the programme was a product of its time was true, but it was still unacceptable. Far from being wholesome entertainment, audiences were exposed to passive racism through their TV screens.

I had been blind to what was happening. In the same way I gave no thought to the fact that some children were given gollies, a type of rag doll, as an alternative to a teddy bear. These dolls had jet-black skin, white-rimmed eyes, red lips, and frizzy hair and were part of the general racist indoctrination that was so prevalent at the time. The image of the golly was trademarked and used to advertise *Robertson's* jam and shredded marmalade. Gollies on jar labels could be collected, saved, and then sent away in exchange for enamel badges. I collected for an enamel badge of a golly throwing darts.

When eventually legislation to outlaw race discrimination was put before Parliament in 1968, the fires of disharmony were stoked once more. Again, the focus was on the Black Country. Wolverhampton's MP Enoch Powell made his infamous 'Rivers of Blood' speech calling for the repatriation of immigrants. Racial harmony took another knock as protesters, including London dockworkers, took to the streets in support of Powell's idea. Emerging black comedian Lenny Henry joked that he was happy to take a fee to go home as the bus fare to Dudley was not that much. Of course, this was more like gallows humour. There was a lot of hurt and much damage done because of Powell's intervention. Powell himself was dismissed from the Conservative shadow cabinet, and his political career went into decline thereafter.

You have no choice about where you are born and raised and little control over the influences that are around you. At one level I am very fortunate not to have lived in a place where racial hatred was overt and unpleasant. I may have been privileged in this respect, but I am hurt that the Black Country became a focus for discrimination, most notably in Smethwick in 1964 and then through Wolverhampton MP Enoch Powell in 1968. Most of all I feel cheated. I feel cheated that I went along with watching TV programmes such as *The Black and White Minstrel Show*. Then there was the golly enamel badge, and the fact that a golly was a friend of Noddy in the Enid Blyton books that were so apparent in my infancy. My goldfish bowl was polluted, and I never realised it.

# Chapter Sixteen

## *When cash was king*

It is a sad indictment of our society that despite its relative affluence food banks are necessary in order that some families can have enough to eat. Frighteningly, food poverty even extends to some who are working. At the same time food finds its way into landfill from some supermarkets and households, often discarded for going beyond its 'use by' date.

The extent of food poverty in the fifties and sixties was not highlighted in the same way, but the malnourishment of children attending school was, in some cases, all too obvious[97]. It was a time pre-dating 'best before' and 'use by' dates, when how something looked or smelt were the only measures. Back then, food purchases were the preserve of women who often shopped daily and were already experienced in dealing with the shortages and tribulations that rationing had previously caused.

This was also a time before credit cards were introduced, and for many there was the temptation to enter into a hire purchase (HP) agreement to buy expensive household items like furniture. In our house, 'getting stuff on the never, never' was shunned. Instead, enough money was saved first before a purchase could be made. Despite this, Mom had both *Littlewoods* and *Freemans* catalogues[98] which sat alongside the telephone directory in the hall. These thick volumes contained glossy colour images of things like clothes that could be acquired by return of post and be paid for by posting off weekly amounts. The catalogues had succeeded where HP had not, and credit had got in through our back door.

---

97  See references to school milk in Chapter 7.

98  Shockingly for an impressionable boy they included pictures of real women modelling underwear and swimming costumes!

Britain's first credit card was not introduced until 1966 and debit cards over twenty years later[99]. This meant that the only cashless transactions that could be conducted involved writing a paper cheque. Not wishing to be troubled with these, many shops and all independent traders operated a cash-only policy. Most blue-collar and other weekly paid workers received their pay in cash in any case. (Friday was the usual payday, a day when brown pay-packets abounded, complete with holes punched on one side to evidence the presence of bank notes.) White collar workers were, by comparison, paid monthly either by a single cheque or through a transfer to their personal bank accounts. For those who did have an account, there was a need to go to a bank and find a way of cashing the monthly cheque.

Bills for fuel usage, rates[100] and water arrived in the post. Mom dealt with these with a carefully written cheque, which was signed with a flourish and posted back the next day. Although Dad was salaried, Mom still operated on a weekly system. Drawing cash from the bank for the week, she would make provision for up-coming and one-off items of expenditure by sitting at a bureau and deliberately placing notes and coins into different boxes and glass tumblers labelled with things like 'house insurance', 'hair', 'Christmas' and 'boys' shoes'. Once done, the cash left over was there for the weekly shop.

Dad earned a good income, but Mom continued to be frugal and make the most of what was at hand. The highlight of her endeavours came every evening when we sat down to eat a low cost but filling two course meal. Rationing and food and other shortages had bred a 'make do and mend' approach to everyday life that Mom thrived on, and beyond baking and cooking she could also sew, knit, mend and darn clothing.

---

99  The first cash machine appeared in 1967.
100  Now council tax.

Mom made good use of the local shops, making visits with her favourite shopping bag, a purse full of cash and very often a shopping list she had written the night before. At the time there used to be two rows of shops on the estate, one at the bottom of the road and a second a ten-minute walk away in Redwood Road.

Of the closest shops to home, two stick in my memory. Both were packed to the rafters with interesting merchandise. The first functioned as a newsagent, tobacconist and confectioners combined. The shop's stock of goods included something of a 'crossover' for their younger clientele. Here it was possible to buy packs of white sweets shaped as 'cigarette' sticks tipped with red colour or liquorice moulded into the shape of a smoking pipe. Countless children mimicked adults smoking before gobbling their smoking props down. I know from personal experience that maximum effect was only possible in colder weather when the breath was visible in the frosty air. Dad had gone through a stage of smoking small cigars called *Café Crème*, which came in a small metal tin and one of smoking a pipe, so the shop was of particular interest to him. Back then pipe smoking was much more common than it is today. At the time, an expert in a scientific or specialist field was invariably referred to as a 'boffin'. The popular image of a boffin was of a reflective, pipe-smoking genius unhurriedly engaging in higher-level thinking. Most men who wanted to project such an image chose a pipe over cigarettes. A case in point was Harold Wilson, the then Labour Party leader. Wilson was the most successful politician of the era, leading his party to four general election victories and serving as Prime Minister for eight years[101]. Nowadays, political minders and spin doctors are commonplace, but it was something of a novelty at the time that Wilson's external image was so carefully managed. Photo opportunities were used to portray him, pipe in hand or quietly puffing away, as a reliable, thoughtful family man. Churchill used to have his cigars,

---

101  This at the time was a peacetime record.

which were affordable by the privileged few, while Wilson by comparison had his homely pipe.

Today it is possible to sell unwanted items on-line. Long before the internet, this particular shop operated an equivalent system whereby postcards were stuck to the glass on the door and shop window. I got my first pair of football boots by following up on a card with the words 'boys second-hand football boots for sale' written in block capitals. The boots were pocket money affordable and fitted. Black/brown in colour with protected toes, the sides reached as far as the top of my ankles. They were heavy to wear, bore little relation to what professionals were wearing at the time, and belonged to an earlier era. Despite this they were boots, real boots, football boots. Boots that needed cleaning after use, boots with plentiful laces, boots that needed Dubbin wax to protect and waterproof the leather. Boots that needed looking after, just like Dad did with his shoes.

When comedian Ronnie Barker created the seventies sitcom *Open All Hours*, he could easily have had the next shop in the row in mind. This was Pimm's hardware and general store, where Mom had a Saturday job for a while. The shop offered a cornucopia of everyday and more obscure but potentially useful items. The possibility of using the concrete steps in front of the store was seized as a means of displaying some of the items on offer, such as mops, buckets, brushes, shovels, door mats and bins full of dusters, cleaning materials and bars of soap. Before the close of business or when rain threatened, the shop assistants would carry these items back inside.

Stepping over the threshold of the store, the shopper was met with a distinctive smell with notes of linseed oil, paraffin, strong detergent, and scented soap. The shop was the go-to place for loose paraffin and oil to fuel portable domestic heaters, which were commonplace as no one on the estate had central heating. We used a tall cylindrical paraffin heater upstairs to take the chill off the bedrooms before retiring to bed. Later on we had a pink electric blanket that warmed the bed directly rather than the room.

Today there is still a row of shops on Redwood Road. Here the residents of Yew Tree estate might take advantage of one of two general stores, a computer repair shop, a fish and chip shop, a fruit and vegetable store, a takeout cafe, a hairdresser, a barber shop, or a chemist. For locals, these shops represent a convenient asset.

Of all these shops, only the chemist was trading on the estate in the late fifties and sixties. (The idea of taking food or drink out of a café to consume elsewhere was alien, and the notion of computers in a domestic setting was a space age fantasy in any case.) I only remember three of the shops that first stood on the Redwood Road site, but each one offered an insight into a bygone era.

The first was a specialist wool shop. I would accompany Mom as she visited for new supplies for an upcoming task, or some new knitting pattern or different-sized needles. A brass bell behind the door announced our arrival on entry, but despite this the shop held little interest for me. What I remember most is that the owner felt the need to wear a knitted cardigan, either in a weird style or disgusting colour combination or sometimes both.

Next door the chemist shop was guarded by two competing charity box figures perhaps three or four feet high. One featured a schoolchild in leg irons representing those suffering from cerebral palsy. The forlorn figure invited donations to the Spastics Society, now known as Scope[102], through a slot in his head. The rival collection box featured the children's puppet Sooty holding a box with a coin slot for a charity for the blind. At least Sooty had a money box to hold. The poor schoolchild was burdened with not only leg irons but also a hole in his head to take the

---

102 The newer name for the charity is infinitely more subtle and sensitive, but is it too obscure in signalling the reason for the charity?

coins on offer. (The burden of missing arms for the Venus de Milo statue seems by comparison to be a lighter weight to bear.)

Inside the dimly lit shop, there were strange, unidentifiable smells and shelves tightly packed with bottles of branded products. A large polished dark wood counter shared floor space with a cast iron penny-operated weighing machine. From the other side of the counter, it was possible to catch glimpses of a chemist in the backroom concocting remedies and potions. The chemist was a true boffin. (Much later I discovered the utility of locally made jars of smelly, milky white liquid that football teams shared as a leg rub before matches in chilly weather.) It was in this shop that prescriptions written by GPs were exchanged for remedies at a modest cost. A Conservative government introduced prescription charges shortly before I was born in 1952 at a rate of one shilling (12½ pence) per item, which equates to just over £4 today[103]. While shoppers waited for the prescription to be made up the temptation for an impulse buy was obvious. Maybe cod liver oil supplements, or a packet of Teddy Gray's herbal remedy tablets, or a bottle of the sugary thick rosehip syrup meant to help children fend off colds? A huge metal cash register dominated the counter. The cost of individual transactions was input on what looked like typewriter keys by the shop assistant. When totalled there would be a pinging noise and a cash draw would fly open. The bill would be displayed to the shopper in the small window at the top of the machine and would be settled in cash.

The butcher's shop was equally fascinating, but this time the shop was very light and airy. Walking through the front door was not straightforward as vertical plastic flaps and fly paper needed to be navigated. Once inside the shopper was confronted by sawdust on the floor and the sight of men in

---

103 The issue of charging for prescriptions was such a contentious one that it had led to the resignation of the father of the NHS, Nye Bevan, from the Labour Government a year previous.

blooded white aprons working on animal carcasses with tools that looked as if they had been borrowed from Dad's shed. Seeing half a pig's head on the side was a gruesome, disturbing, but fascinating thing to spot. The butchers would break off from their tasks to serve customers. Part of the routine involved taking fat pencils from behind their ears to add the cost of purchases using huge sheets of white paper. The paper doubled as both a receipt and wrapping paper for the meat. The same men who welded saws, choppers and knives switched to the mathematics of three columns of pounds, shillings, and pence effortlessly and expertly with no calculator or cash register in sight.

Family-run and small businesses such as those represented by the shops on the estate are today under pressure. They are being squeezed by supermarkets that allow the shopper to choose for themselves meat, groceries, and basic branded chemist shop remedies all in one place. Supermarkets did not catch on until the late sixties and beyond. The public, it seemed, preferred to make purchases from several local shops over the course of a week. Food rationing was introduced during the Second World War and only finished eighteen months before I was born when the government finally lifted restrictions on the sale and purchase of meat and bacon. For a decade and a half, therefore, the nation had grown accustomed to holding ration books and expecting a daily replenishment of food shelves. Queuing for food, exchanging news, opinions and stories with shopkeepers and bystanders became a near daily occurrence. Rationing apart, fresh meat, unless salted or put in a cool larder or pantry, could go off and be wasted as refrigerators were by no means common[104], making a daily shop more important.

---

104 By 1961 half of the country's households owned a television set but only one in five had a refrigerator, making near daily food purchases a necessity for eighty per cent of the population.

I once saw a programme on television, possibly *Tomorrow's World*, that suggested that in the future we would no longer need to waste time eating, instead we would be able to take a daily mix of protein and other tablets. Thankfully, this never came about. Food is too important, representing an opportunity for gathering, sharing and communion. As a family we always ate together at the dinner table, never in front of the television. It was here that we heard about Dad's working day, his arguments, his successes, and the people he worked with. When regaling us with his anecdotes, a vein twitched on the side of his head as he galloped through his plate of food. I suppose Dad needed praise, an acknowledgement of achievement, and encouragement and would seek it around the family table.

At that time there were no fast-food restaurants or pub grub options, and the only form of takeaway was to be found at a fish and chip shop. (It is significant that the government, when making exceptions to rationing, identified beer, bread, and food from the 'chippy' as off ration.) Corner cafes were the refuge of those far from home, and restaurants were for the monied upper classes. We never ate out as a family.

Yew Tree estate may have evolved its own culture, but it was no isolated community immune from visitors. Households expected twice daily postal deliveries, and in an era where print assumed much greater significance in communicating issues of international, national, and local importance, a morning and late afternoon delivery of newspapers also operated.

With the limited nature of shops on the estate there was a constant stream of vendors in the street. Weary tradespeople in crumpled suits burdened with suitcases of tightly packed merchandise systematically knocked every door in the hope of a sale. Mom occasionally bought dusters and cleaning products from door-to-door salesmen.

Some houses would take a weekly delivery of bottled mineral water and fizzy fruit drinks. In exchange, empty but clean bottles would be returned on the van. A similar system operated for a Birmingham-based brewery *Davenports* that specialised in home delivery of beer, but this was only an occasional visitor to the estate. Once a week, someone sold wet fish from a refrigerated van strategically parked about the estate. Nearby, Nan bought provisions from someone called Andy, who packed an old van to the gunnels with groceries before taking it around houses where there was a predominance of pensioners.

The sight and sound of the 'rag un bone mon' was a thing to behold. The sounding of an old foghorn and cry of 'rag, bone' would announce the arrival of an open backed van piled high with old rubbish. Despite the name, rags and bones were not on these traders' agenda. The real interest was in items like old prams, bikes, white goods, damaged saucepans, and the like. In return they might give away a balloon to any interested child. Scrapyards were the life blood of Black Country steelworks, which consumed ferocious quantities of ferrous scrap and street collections helped feed the habit. There were two or three different scrap merchants who patrolled the estate.

Apart from their trade, they all had one thing in common. That thing was tattoos. Smudgy blue tattoos dripping with dull red hearts and full of images of snakes and curvy women. One had tattoos of swallows on the back of his hands. My sons' generation have made tattooing de rigueur, but this was not the case when I was a kid. Today both my sons are well and truly inked, and so are their partners. The artwork on their arms, chests, hands, and legs would have aroused a great deal of interest and comment back then. This was an era when tattoos were rarely seen on men and never on women. Those tattooed would be restricted to a narrow group of men such as fairground attendants, former merchant seamen and rag and bone men. (In an earlier generation, a fairground attraction may include the rare opportunity to view a tattooed lady.)

New days were not announced by birdsong so much as the sound of the delivery of milk to doorsteps. The milk float was battery driven and near silent, but the clinking bottles and rattling crates were noisy, as was the milkman himself. It seemed as if part of the milkman's training involved mastering the art of whistling in a piercing fashion and extending and contorting the knuckles of each hand to carry several pint-sized milk bottles. Normally milk was pasteurised, but a few households preferred sterilised milk, which appeared on doorsteps in taller, thinner bottles. As mid-morning approached, the man selling bread would do his rounds, carrying bread over his arm in a wicker basket. Wearing a brown overall and socks and sandals, he often stopped for a chat with Mom. Both the milkman and the baker worked for 'the Co-op'.

The country's Co-operative movement can be traced back to the protective working-class collectives that grew as a response to the damaging effect of the Industrial Revolution on jobs and in-dividual well-being. When I was a child *The Walsall and District Co-operative Society* seemed to have tentacles everywhere and was strongly supported by Mom and Dad in terms of banking, insurances, milk, and bread delivery and occasionally clothing and grocery purchases. It had many branches, the nearest being the grocery shop in the Delves area of Walsall. Profits were dis-tributed to members in the form of dividends. Both of my par-ents knew their divi number by heart and recited it when hand-ing over their cash (it incorporated a string of numbers that coincided with Dad's old army number). These numbers were recorded in a carbonised book and, somehow, the dividend due was calculated by the society. The exciting part was the payout of hard cash at the counter in Walsall town centre twice a year[105].

The country may have had the figurehead of Elizabeth II as queen, but everyday life was governed by cash. Cash was king. The Co-op divi was a welcome bonus on the side.

---

105 A practice that only ceased in 1968 with the introduction of Co-op saving stamps instead.

# Chapter Seventeen

*Art for art's sake, shopping for goodness' sake*

Letchworth, Hertfordshire, was the world's first Garden City when it was built in 1903. Others were to follow. Garden cities were constructed with the stated intention of combining the best of town and country. Yew Tree Estate, by comparison, had no such design brief. It was simply neither town nor country, and to experience either of these extremes meant a trip from the estate. Apart from the dubious attraction of football matches at Fellows Park, travels centred on Walsall town centre with Mom. Geographically, West Bromwich was about the same distance, but this was never really a destination of choice for tribal reasons. Venturing further afield out of the Black Country, Birmingham offered the promise of something different. It involved journeying through an alien landscape of dark, dilapidated housing and dirty industry to a city centre with grand buildings that reflected a heritage of past civic pride and wealth.

For a while I attended West Bromwich School of Art and Design. The local education authority was running a scheme whereby each junior school could nominate one pupil to attend a Saturday morning class, and I was the choice of Yew Tree Junior School. I enjoyed the experience of the bus ride on my own to a cavernous red bricked municipal building where the ceilings were high, corridors echoed, and huge heavy doors had brass fittings. Here I encountered enthusiastic art teachers who challenged their young pupils to really look, reflect and then use various materials to create different pieces of art. The experience challenged my understanding. Up until that point, art was, for me, the production of a lifelike scene, rectangular in shape and capable of being mounted on a wall. Once on the wall it became a magic decorative illusion as if it were a window of a view of something going on the other side of the wall. The experience of the art school allowed me to rethink what I understood by the term 'art'.

My 'magic window' understanding of art had been shaped by earlier trips to Birmingham. There was a period when Dad had to work on Saturday mornings, and Mom spotted an opportunity for a low-cost break from the routine. So, the whole family would rise early, and Dad would drop the three of us off on the way into the office in the nearby suburb of Edgbaston. He would then collect us about lunchtime. This gave us a few hours to visit either the art gallery, or the science museum[106]. Here we were treated to free education and culture, and it was not even a school day! The art gallery was a wondrous place where huge oil pictures in heavy frames told stories, some mythical and otherworldly, while others asked questions of the viewer. Threateningly life-like figures in paintings made direct eye contact as they towered above me. Some magic windows made me drop my voice in reverence. Was I undergoing a quasi-spiritual experience, or was it that the building had the feeling of a huge library about it?

One category of painting involved biblical scenes. Here beautifully depicted melancholy characters looked downhearted by the prospect of being peered at by intruders from the Yew Tree Estate. Their demeanour never seemed joyful in any way or even angry, they always seemed sad and thoughtful. Resplendent figures in shiny silken garments were captured in a moment of time

---

106 Brother Tim seemed more interested in the science museum where there were bits of working machines, various engines and, in keeping with the period, far from interactive displays. It was more a collection of historically significant artefacts boxed in glass prisons or protected behind rope barriers. Unfortunately, this was only of passing interest to me which was a pity given the industrial heritage and innovation of Birmingham and the Black Country.

against a landscape I naturally assumed was the Holy Land. Little did I know that I was seeing fifteenth century Italian scenery!

A further type of magic window involved what I learned much later were Pre-Raphaelite paintings. Full of incredibly detailed and realistic backgrounds, they often featured alluring raven-haired beauties with a certain look about them. Did these female figures wrestle to extricate themselves from the canvas and step through the elaborate frames when no one was looking? If so, their facial features suggested a promise of spice and maybe a little temper. These ladies could never be mistaken for the Virgin Mary in religious paintings.

Then there was a different category of picture altogether. Here artists used the magic window as an excuse for depicting fleshy subjects, often a little dumpy and always pink in colour. There must have been a worthy reason for the painting, but I could not help thinking it was more a hugely elaborate, old-fashioned version of the calendar that hung in the Delves barber's shop. Was this old-time titillation for patrons with too much money and too little taste?

While I was viewing magic windows there was something of a revolution in the art world going on. Many artists, most notably Pablo Picasso, led the way with his multiple innovative painting styles, sculptures, and ceramics. Meanwhile fellow Spaniard Salvador Dali and other surrealists were producing haunting nightmarish compositions[107]. There was no pretence that the image reflected the world the other side of the wall, indeed the window was dispensed with completely. Meanwhile pop art was

---

107 Both men were Spanish but shared quite different political views. Picasso was under self-imposed exile in France because of the rule of the fascist General Franco in his homeland. Dali was said to admire the Nazis and remained in Spain.

emerging from America, most famously including the works of Andy Warhol, who held a mirror up to a world increasingly concerned with consumerism. These works, or any like them, never found their way into the Birmingham art gallery. Despite this our time was well spent on a Saturday morning. The variety of magic windows could be viewed for free, each pointing to a shared culture and offering a vision of a world, normally a beautiful one. There was an undeniable awe and opulence in many of the paintings and a strange reverence around the place. Not every work of art was to my taste, but it would seem shocking to think that these paintings would be simply torn to pieces just because of that. Or that pottery would be deliberately smashed, artefacts of the past defaced, or a bonfire made of books from the nearby municipal library. Yet this is exactly what was happening in China about this time.

The People's Republic of China was founded in 1949 and initially tolerated any form of art so long as it did not criticise the state and served the people (however that was defined). By the sixties, however, one of the revolution's leaders, Mao Zedong, was becoming agitated by how the country was shaping up under communism. Economic failures had led to a great famine, and he did want the country to develop in the same way as that other communist giant, the Soviet Union. Taking a more direct role, Mao oversaw a Cultural Revolution[108] in 1966. Chinese urban youths functioned as agents of change to purge the country of 'impure elements', specifically its ties to the country's tradition and past, including its customs, culture, habits, and ideas. The old order was said to be an obstacle to development. Gangs of youngsters, known as the Red Guards, were given free rein by the Chinese Red Army to implement the new initiative. Apart from the wanton destruction of objects and materials, they mercilessly victimised, humiliated and killed any individual

---

108 Or more properly the Great Proletarian Cultural Revolution.

who was perceived as being elitist, intellectual, or bourgeois. The quest was to purge the country of all elements associated with tradition and capitalism. In the process economic activity stalled, over a million were murdered, and invaluable historical and cultural objects were destroyed. The Cultural Revolution continued up until Mao's death in 1976.

While revolutionary forms of art and the Cultural Revolution were global issues, our family had the more pressing concern of shopping requirements that had to be addressed. Today the presence of competing town centre malls, out-of-town retail parks and on-line shopping provide the shopper with a vast choice of products and suppliers. Back then things were much more limited and straightforward. The paucity of shops locally meant there might be a need to go to a town for something specialist or different. Walsall town centre fitted the bill. Art supplies could only be obtained from *Gadsbys* in Bradford Street, sporting requirements were only met in *Lawrence and Platers* of Ablewell Street, and school uniforms were only available from *Buxton and Bonnets* situated in the Digbeth Arcade.

Although tobacco-based products are currently widely available, successive campaigns highlight the dangers of smoking, all packs carry warnings and advertising is curbed. Back then there were no warnings and a shared general ignorance of the damage that can be caused by smoking. Movies almost celebrated smoking, and footballers lent their names to advertising in newspapers and matchday programmes. Photographs of stars of the era, like crooner Frank Sinatra and film stars James Dean and Humphrey Bogart regularly appeared with an obligatory cigarette in the corner of their mouths. Some brands encouraged smoking by including collectable cards on a variety of subjects such as animals, footballers, or flags of the world. It seemed to be compulsory for passengers to smoke on the top deck of a bus. Workmen took timeout for a 'fag break'. Offices were a fog of smoke. Royalty did it, sportsmen did it, actors did it, so did politicians. The very choice of cigarette brand represented a statement to the outside world. So, for instance *Senior Service* projected a military man's choice, *Marlboro* suggested an adventurous cowboy spirit, *Park Lane* was for an everyday person while *Woodbine* was for the working-class man, and so on.

Such was the demand that specialist tobacconist shops operated, one being on the Bridge in Walsall town centre. The tiny shop had a polished dark wood counter and elegant brass fittings. Opening the heavy door and venturing into the premises, the shopper was met with a heady aroma of sweet smelling, sickly fragrances. Here was an enticingly glamorous world of loose tobacco in jars, elegantly coloured tins, no end of pipes and pipe cleaners and wooden boxes containing huge cigars that would have done Churchill proud. On the walls, metal plates advertised not run-of-the-mill cigarettes like *Park Drive*, *Woodbine* and *Capstan* but exotically named and illustrated brands.

A stroll along the main streets of Walsall town centre confirmed just how different it was from the estate. Pedestrianised areas were not in vogue, instead there were beautifully constructed arcades and elegant buildings. The George Hotel on the Bridge was a large, impressive structure, and a little further along there were the fine Edwardian-fronted shops on Bradford Street, which boasted balconies at the upper level. The weekly newspaper, the *Walsall Observer*, operated from one of these premises. These led on to the grand looking Town Hall in Lichfield Street, which was directly opposite the Co-operative departmental store and Walsall Mutual Building Society office. Around the corner were the public baths that boasted a brine bath, introduced because of their perceived health benefits.

The legacy of Walsall corporation's trolley buses could still be seen in the overhead electricity cables around Walsall's town centre streets. Trolley buses first operated in Berlin as long ago as 1882 but were only taken up as a form of transport in this country thirty years later. In Walsall, trolley buses, which had replaced trams as a form of public transport, were now being phased out in favour of double decker buses, which mirrored the shape and blue livery of their predecessors. At their height of popularity, Walsall corporation operated sixty trolley buses and, for over forty years offered quick, quiet, dependable, and comfortable rides to paying passengers. On the day the last trolley bus ran between Bloxwich and the town centre two and a half miles away, Mom took us for a ride, and we sat on the top deck. I meant to keep the ticket but somehow lost it. Today operators are being pressured to replace their vehicles with low-emission equivalents. It is ironic that the discarded trolley buses were less polluting and harmful to the environment than their diesel-run successors.

If it was market day, the outdoor market offered additional noise, colour, and bustle, just as it had for the past seven hundred years or so. Market traders shouted encouragements to shoppers from under the canvas coverings stretched over the stall's metal struts. Other stallholders crouched like coiled springs behind their timber trestle tables, ready to pounce on the notes and coins offered to them. These traders uniformly wore sporran money bags just below their belts and, in colder weather, also shared a preference for wearing woollen gloves with the fingers removed.

The market experience involved walking steeply downhill over a cobbled surface and passing through a series of inducements to part with your money. Suddenly indispensably useful items, along with the temptations of knock down prices and one-off bargains made competing demands upon the wallet or purse.

'... doe forget to buy these bab before you go um.'

'... yow'll pay much more for these in Brummigum.'

'... this is today's price mate, next wick it'll be more.'

The experience began just below the steps of St. Matthews church at the top of the hill. One trader cut huge sections of foam rubber to any size requested. Here 'make do and menders' saw the opportunity to replace their lifeless settee cushions or repair car seats. Opposite someone fried savoury potato snacks not unlike a warmed up prototype 'cheesy quavers' in boiling oil. Sold in white paper bags the experience left grease and warmth on the buyer's fingers. Moving down, there were bric-a-brac stalls, one selling curios, postcards, cigarette and tea cards, old war medals and memorabilia. Then there was a shoes and slipper stall, another selling wool and patterns, zips, and buttons, one selling gloves and jumpers, one selling toys, and at the midway point local character Syd Wright had his crockery stall. Further down, the bottom section of the market broadened out and included a stall selling loose chocolate and sweets, including honeycomb and liquorish misshapes.

A record stall sold cheap long-playing albums by artists no one had ever heard of with unlikely titles like *Digits McGhee plays Honky Tonk* and had boxes of second-hand singles. These records had dropped out of the charts and had been retired from pub jukeboxes. Now a little worn and warped, they were looking to be rehoused. Here was the possibility of owning three minutes of catchy music and the surprise track on the B side at pocket money prices. These stiff seven-inch black vinyl gems just needed a plastic adaptor fitting to the hole punched in the middle to allow it to be played at 45 revolutions per minute (unlike the 33rpm of the albums). Once played at home, the stylus rode the warped surface like a rowing boat fighting through an ocean of waves.

One stall specialised in items for the home that were kitsch even by the standards of the day. There were framed prints of tearful children with oversized eyes and dogs wearing clothes engaged in adult activities like playing snooker and smoking. Then there was John Constable's Hay Wain taken to a different level. Framed reproductions with an eerie yellow tinge were available in virtually every size, some with clocks and barometers in the top right-hand corner. The stall was completed with a variety of glass ornaments in figures like clowns and ballet dancers, pottery shire horses and brandy glasses with porcelain cats attempting to climb inside.

The next stall sold gents ties and shirts, some packaged together in cellophane wrappers ready for gifting to some doubtless disappointed Walsall man on their special occasion. Nearby there was the distinctive smell of authentic leather from a stall that nodded at the town's heritage by selling bags, wallets, purses, and belts. Unpromisingly there was the competing aroma of wet fish from the stall opposite. Then there were stalls offering towels, tea towels and bedding; one sold cheap jewellery, another home hair dyes, combs, brushes, tights and so on. Finally, the shopper had the opportunity to rid themselves of coins from their pockets by buying a freshly baked loaf of bread or a bargain bag of broken biscuits.

Nearby there was a plant and flower shop where Mom would sometimes stop to buy her boys a miniature cactus each. This was something to keep and value. A plant of my own in a colourful plastic pot that looked like a junior relative of something that appeared regularly on cowboy films. The plant was difficult to kill, even through negligence, and it could wonderfully and unexpectedly throw out shoots and explode into flowers every now and then.

Opposite the plant and flower shop was *Hawkins*, a drapery supplier and a truly memorable shop. Brightly coloured lengths of material lay on huge desks and oversized scissors and tape measures in feet and inches abounded. The quirkiest thing however was an antiquated cash collection system featuring brass parts and overhead pulleys that echoed a much earlier era. The system still had relevance and value. With the handling of a lot of cash and its retention in cash tills on shop counters, the risk of loss or theft was obvious. *Hawkins*, along with older Co-op stores, used a system whereby bank notes were packed in a brass capsule, a handle on a chain was pulled (not unlike a water closet) and magically an overhead mini rail system despatched the cargo safely to a remote cashier's office away from the shop floor.

The visit to the market was concluded by the sight of a piece of public art, an elegant bronze statue of Sister Dora. Sister Dora Pattison was Walsall's own local version of Florence Nightingale and even had the local General Hospital named after her. Her statue gazed wistfully away from the market and the George Hotel behind her towards Park Street and the railway station beyond. It is anyone's guess what she would make of the changes to the town today in response to changed shopping trends.

# Chapter Eighteen

*Hair raising experiences*

Just about every lady I knew went to a great deal of trouble with their hair. Some younger women might sport a beehive hairstyle, others an elaborate back combed and thickly lacquered coiffure.

This made them look much taller than they were, especially if they wore high-heeled shoes. It was not unusual to see women of the period in rollers and a headscarf getting on with jobs around the home before brushing their hair out. A lady came round every other Friday evening to put a colour on Mom's hair before 'setting it' (whatever that entailed). Nan used to go to the hairdressers to have a 'shampoo and set'. Following her fortnightly outing, she would emerge from 'Maureen's' with a freshly spruced up, snow white, meringue hair topping. The whole creation received protection from a type of rainhat surely fashioned out of old net curtains. Other ladies of her age had their white hair tinted with curious light blue, rose or purple shades, doubtless inspiring the paint company *Dulux* to introduce an off-white colour range!

For the most part, men's hair of the period was short and unremarkable. Restrictions imposed by the military[109] had produced a legacy of no-nonsense 'short back and sides' haircuts. Most also plastered what remained of their hair with grease. England captain Johnny Haynes is remembered as the first English professional footballer to be paid £100 a week following the abolition of the wage cap in 1961. However, he also fronted newspaper and television advertisements for *Brylcreem* hair cream ('all your hair needs for health and appearance'). To help combat the potential greasy damage to settees and armchairs, living rooms

---

109  The last call ups for national service ended on the last day of 1960.

of the period contained strange ornamental towels placed on head rests called antimacassars.

The long hair favoured by the American hippy subculture had yet to penetrate Britain to any degree. Similarly, the appearance of pop stars like the Beatles and the Rolling Stones in the mid-sixties had yet to make an impact on the estate's male residents. In Walsall town centre there might be the sight of someone with a heavy fringe as a nod to the emerging trend. At the same time there might be an odd teddy boy or two[110] favouring the previous decade's trend with longer, slicked-back hair and extended side boards. The teddy boys seemed a breed apart. They had trousers that were a bit too tight and a bit too short. Their jackets were a bit too bright and a bit too long, and their shoes were like no other, being chunky and called 'brothel creepers'. Yet the complete look, including hair, seemed to work even if it was not cool anymore. There were also a few young men whose hair suggested they believed they were the Black Country's answer to film star Tony Curtis or rock 'n roller Elvis Presley.

As a child I hated having my hair cut. I have not changed much since. I knew that the sight of an illuminated red and white pole outside a shop meant an unpleasant experience was waiting on  the other side of the door. The sensation of hair down my back, the itchy irritation on my collar and the possibility of the bloody mess of clippers taking the top off a mole on my neck was bad enough. There was also the obligation to engage in one-to-one chitchat with the barber. Having a haircut was infinitely more unpleasant than a wet Sunday afternoon or a visit to the dentist.

---

110 Teddy Boys took their name from wearing clothes influenced by styles from the Edwardian period. With a love for American rock 'n roll music they represented a subculture of the fifties.

When we could put it off no longer, Mom would walk her sons over the Common to the barber's shop, which was situated on the corner opposite the local Co-op store in the Delves. Mom would make small talk over the noise coming from the chunky portable transistor radio while I waited in silence like someone on death row. Sitting there alongside yesterday's newspapers and sweet wrappers, I faked disinterest in the unsuitable calendar with its glossy flesh screaming 'look at me'. The calendar shared the wall with certificates and pictures of men who had just had a haircut. There were shiny taps and sinks in the shop, but these were never used for anything other than filling the barber's kettle. I would eventually climb into a chair that was pumped up for height and have a gown tucked around me. I then suffered the ignominy of seeing the systematic butchery of my hair while unwillingly engaging in a stilted conversation with a stranger. Then a handheld mirror was angled to give a view of just how bad it looked from the back. The requirement was to say that the look was fine and 'thank you' before spending the rest of the day trying to remove loose hair from my neck and back. When Mom thought we were old enough, I was entrusted with the money for two haircuts, and Tim and I would trudge unwillingly to the shop.

At one point Mom attempted the job herself, reasoning it would save a few shillings, and what harm could it do anyway? She acquired a strange stubby combing device that she had seen advertised in a magazine. The idea was that the comb, which concealed a razor blade, glided over the hair then, with a shake of the head, clumps of hair would fall to the ground to reveal a stylish, professional haircut. That was the theory anyway. The experience turned out to be even worse than a visit to the barber's shop with the added peril of the possibility of real damage being done to my neck, ears and indeed anywhere on my upper torso.

On a few occasions Dad would take matters into his own hands, and the three males of the household would embark on an outing to  a small place just off the high street in West Bromwich. The journey from the estate to West Bromwich offered unusual viewing experiences. There was an impossibly narrow single lane bridge at Friar Park, a road that regularly flooded under a railway bridge (with an appropriately named 'Navigation' pub marking the spot), and a deep sand quarry just outside the Stone Cross. In the summer months the flooded pit became festooned with children in swimming costumes playing, sliding, splashing and, in some cases, diving. These were days before health and safety regulations and evidently also the days before common sense applied. West Bromwich had its gala baths, Walsall had its brine baths, Wolverhampton had Tettenhall Pool, but the go to place for children from the area playing hooky[111] on a sweltering summer's day was Stone Cross quarry pool.

Arriving at our destination, the small shop looked unpromising from the outside. It was difficult to see through the dirty front window due to condensation that had been produced by a smelly paraffin heater. For those brave enough to step over the threshold there was a remarkable sight. It was as if the dust had just settled after an atomic explosion in a bicycle graveyard. Here old, abandoned, and worn-out bikes were being given a second life by being heavily greased and refitted with new gears, brakes, saddles, and whatever it took to get them on the road again. There were bike frames of all sizes, grease guns, tools, and parts old and new everywhere.

The shop's owner, Mr Talis, who seemed to know Dad well, would break off from working on a cycle before getting on with the business of cutting hair. He would knock the dust off a chair with the back of a gown and produce an electric shaver. Even though Mr Talis smelt of a combination of cigarettes and grease, this was a

---

111 Playing hooky is a schoolchild's expression for playing truant, my
    school friends used the term 'wagging it' also.

better experience and system than a normal barber's shop. The operation was considerably swifter and did not involve all that nonsense with conversation and mirrors. The job was complete when Mr Tallis pressed a metal comb across the hair line on the nape of my neck and ran a lit taper across it.

'What's that for Dad?'
    'Mr Talis will tell you ...'
    (Mr Talis) 'That will keep the winter out son.'

Dad obviously liked the hybrid barber/bike repairer, and the conversations between the two men were quite entertaining. Dad talked politics and Mr Talis contributed home-spun philosophy interspersed with gossip. He told stories of the unlikely people he had sold his own form of recycled cycles to.

'... last wick there was the Chairman of the Council's Road Safety Committee in here, and while he was here, he said ...'

'... this one bloke came in looking for a bike for his nipper for Christmas, anyrodeup it turns out that he was in the newspaper next wick for ...'

Dad's hair treatment was completed by trimming the worst of the straw from his eyebrows as the two men exchanged more views on issues such as the state of Labour politician Dennis Healey's eyebrows.

Dad passed Mr Talis the money for the work he had done. Mr Talis slipped it into a wooden drawer and picked up a spanner to get back to the job he was working on before we had interrupted him. Stepping back outside the shop the wind felt keen around my ears. It was time to return to the estate and its own form of normality.

It seemed a quirky thing that a barber would double up doing another job, in this case bike repairs, in the lull between customers turning up. There is however some history of extended job descriptions amongst barbers. Several hundred years earlier, they acted as both part-time surgeons and dentists performing tasks like minor surgery, tooth removal, and bloodletting[112]. The blood and bandages inspired poles outside barbers' shops signalled as much. It was an issue that went over my head at the time, but in the fifties and sixties barber shops also sold contraceptives. The enquiry 'would you like anything for the weekend sir?' had a particular meaning at that time. The connotations of such a question in a much earlier period might have implied the requirement for a limb amputation or a tooth extraction!

Today, shoe repairers normally also cut keys which seems a peculiar task combination. Mr Talis' bargain bikes/barber combination was, I suppose, no less strange. One Christmas I received an example of this side-line as a present from Mom and Dad. Of course, there was no safety helmet, no one wore such a thing. One item that was considered vital however was a bell. I liked the pre-loved[113] bike complete with a new bell, and used it a lot, but it always reminded me of having my hair cut. I do not like having my hair cut.

---

112 It was believed that certain illnesses could be cured by the removal of unhealthy blood and body fluids from the patient. Sometimes leeches were used for the purpose.

113 A phrase that seems to have taken root lately. Everyone back then used the term 'second hand' instead.

# GROWING PAINS, PASSIONS AND PUZZLES

# Chapter Nineteen

## *Street life (and a guilty innocent)*

It happened down the street. Cars, motorcycles, and bikes passed by on the road to nowhere of significance. My seniors engaged in sensible, serious adult activities like holding in-depth conversations, window cleaning, washing cars and generally doing important things. Children were active just being children. It all went on down the street.

Down the street, the Common beckoned eager young footballers. By calling at a couple of houses there would be enough for a kickabout. Ian Houghton from around the corner would join me. Brother Tim was always an uncomplaining conscript then along the way was the home of Alan, a classmate and friend. He was likely to play. We sat next to one another at school. Alan came from a Catholic household and was the eldest child of a couple who were unable to speak or hear. Being less than sensitive times, they were referred to as being 'deaf and dumb'. To add to their difficulties, they struggled with literacy. Impressively, Alan unabashed and uncomplainingly stepped into the breach. He read to them all the correspondence they received using his expertise in sign language. He once gave me a spare pocket diary that contained both the British and the American sign language alphabets. There were drawings of contorted fingers representing individual letters from which words and sentences could be constructed. At the time it seemed to me that even if both parties knew the alphabet, the speed of conversation would be at a snail's pace[114]. Yet he managed. In addition to his expertise

---

114 Signing at conferences and on television programmes today seems far less complicated than spelling out every single word with the fingers.

in this special language, Alan also had an ability to calm and deal with his younger brother Tony, who could be quite wild. I never appreciated just how talented he was at the time. I do not think he did either.

Opposite Alan's home lived two more classmates and potential candidates for a kickabout, David and Michael. These identical twins were indistinguishable to everyone except their mother, Muriel. Emotionally and socially the boys were so inseparable that they could have been conjoined. They sat next to one another in class, spent time with one another at breaks and paired off in games lessons. They wore identical clothes. They even joined in with one another's conversations, instinctively knowing what the other was about to say. One story was told of how Michael tumbled from top to bottom of the stairs one day and escaped without so much as a mark. The next day David complained that his back was sore, and afterwards terrible bruises appeared. The tale put a shiver down my spine. Looking back, I should have considered alternative possibilities for such a thing happening. The story could have been exaggerated. Alternatively, the twins could have decided to play a trick on everyone, and it was David who had really tumbled down the staircase. We attended one another's birthday parties (theirs being a joint affair obviously), chatted in the playground, and played football together. I lost touch when my family left the estate. I was told that the twins went on to attend the same secondary school, followed by the same university and then undertook an apprenticeship at the same company. Whether this is true or not, David and Michael are the closest examples I have ever encountered of a single person living a double existence.

The houses in Lilac Avenue had narrow driveways to the gardens and garages[115] at the rear of the property. These driveways

---

115 Nowadays the trend seems to be to keep cars outside overnight, back then virtually every car was housed in a garage.

were shared between two households and were ungated. By walking down the street it was possible to look between the houses and get a glimpse of someone else's life. There might be games being played and laughter, or children being reprimanded, or voices raised in argument. Kids hung about, women pegged washing on lines, and men spent their leisure time either gardening or draped over or under their cars. Men checked tyre pressure and inflated tyres with foot pumps, drained radiators to make way for new anti-freeze mixture, used distilled water to top up batteries, checked spark plug gaps and conducted regular refills of engine oil and radiator water. Then there was the car body to deal with. They would rub down rust, apply filler to body work, spray paint and finally wash and wax their demanding indulgence. The car maintenance routines that seemed so vital then hardly ever seem to be conducted now, or if they are, then it is left to the expertise of a garage.

Nowadays, it is most unlikely that cars will rust to any great degree or fail to start or break down mid-journey[116]. The application of Total Quality Management (TQM) and other quality methods by Japanese car manufacturers and other converts, which really took root in the 1970s, have seen to this. Before then cars of the period were potential rust buckets and far less dependable than they are today. Weekends and evenings therefore involved peering under car bonnets or using imperial-sized spanners and screwdrivers to fix, adjust or improve. The use of the term 'car repairs' today is misleading, with the emphasis being upon a replacement of worn parts. Back then it was about making repairs and, inevitably, some efforts were more successful than others. So, for instance, attempts to remedy a noisy exhaust might involve covering holes in the pipes with an adhesive bandage, welding a metal patch onto a hole or adopting other

---

116 The capability even exists for cars to drive themselves!

Heath Robinson[117] approaches. An evening institute ran at my school with one of the classes being car maintenance. Men also gave one another tips based on first-hand experiences, such as "use your wife's tights to repair a fan belt", "break an egg into a radiator to fix a leak", "cover spark plugs with a tea towel at night to keep the damp out", and so on. Tights? Eggs? Tea towels? I will leave you to judge the validity of the advice that was given.

Men invested time and patience in keeping their object of social status, transport to work and family mobility going. When a car failed to start on a Monday morning, owners must have felt a sense of injustice. In desperation some would turn the engine over repeatedly, hoping that their pampered possession would cough into life before the battery went flat. Sometimes the solution might involve a jump or bump start using the slope of Lilac Avenue, building up a speed and then hoping the car would lurch into responsiveness when the clutch was released. When successful, noxious odours would be belched into the air, and with juddering exhaust pipes, engines would roar like wounded beasts. The first car my parents owned attempted to cover the eventuality that the car may not start by coming complete with a starting handle just below the front number plate. So, with much manual effort, the handle crank might lead to the engine turning over. (Alternatively, it might result in nothing more than dislocation of the shoulder.)

Dad was old school in many ways, believing in structure, order, systems and discipline, everything indeed he had willingly embraced during his time in the army. His appearance mattered, and most evenings he could be found either pressing his work trousers with an iron and wet tea towel or getting a shine on

---

117 William Heath Robinson is best remembered as a cartoonist who, during the first half of the twentieth century, humorously depicted over-elaborate machines, etc., undertaking routine processes or mundane tasks.

his shoes with the help of a tin of *cherry blossom* polish and an old toothbrush. At night every external door and gate had to be locked, double locked and checked in a particular sequence before the keys were returned to their designated hook under the stairs. He kept files of receipts for every payment conceivable and copies of letters he had written. He also maintained a small logbook recording the date, how many gallons of petrol he had bought, the price and the mileage of the car. This he kept in the car's glove compartment. Growing up, the two-minute record-taking after every fill-up seemed normal, and I just assumed everyone did the same. From this unassuming book, Dad was able to quote with authority, 'how many miles to the gallon I got when we went to Blackpool' or that petrol prices had risen by such and such since this time last year.

No one could afford a brand-new car, but the number of households on the estate with access to a vehicle seemed much higher than the national average of one in three. Today vehicle manufacture is a global affair, but at the time it was predominantly national. The insular outlook and xenophobia of the time meant that virtually all foreign cars were treated with suspicion. There was a wide variety of British producers, including the bigger companies like Vauxhall, Ford, and Rootes (which incorporated Hillman, Sunbeam, and Humber cars). The biggest of all was the British Motor Corporation (BMC), which included Austin, Austin-Healey, Morris, MG, Riley, and Wolseley. For richer motorists wanting a luxury saloon or sports car, there was also Bentley, Rover, Triumph, Jaguar and, in a parallel universe somewhere far away from Yew Tree estate, there was Rolls Royce. Of the cars on the estate, the flashiest were Fords. The *Zephyr* and the even bigger *Zodiac* may not have been as iconic as an American 57 *Chevy*, but they could be head turners. Long, wide, and shiny, their names gave a nod to the ongoing space race and their body design was doubtless influenced by comic book images of space craft. Aunty Daisy's son-in-law, John, was a builder who alternated between being out of work and being fully employed and well paid. When in work he would buy a car such as the *Zodiac*, complete with its comfortable looking seats, chrome encased mirrors, body piping and crimped tail fins.

There were a few motorcycles to be seen, some had sidecars attached to their bikes. These were not owned by enthusiasts but by those who lacked the necessary budget for a car or had yet to obtain a full driving licence. As a form of transport, motorcycles seemed to be even more temperamental than cars. Dependent upon their mood they might respond to being kick-started for the umpteenth time by springing forward. If they did, riders had to hang on grimly to a lurching uncaged beast. Alternatively, they might just give a weary cough and go back to sleep, refusing to respond to all attempts to get them to go.

The obvious appetite for personal vehicle ownership coincided with the government's vision for transportation. The completion of the M1 in 1959 gifted the country with its first full-length motorway. The Black Country was first linked to other parts of the country by canals, then railways, now it was the turn of motorways. Linking the midlands to London and the Southeast, the M1 drew fascinated motorists. A family day out could now involve marvelling at the wonder of lengths of no stop, no speed limit stretches of tarmac. This highway came complete with smooth road surfaces, slender bridges, gentle curves, and free emergency telephones. This was a world with an absence of restrictions on the capability of the driver, the use of seat belts, the road worthiness of the vehicles, or the speed of travel. There was no requirement for a vehicle MOT test, alcohol breathalysers had yet to be introduced, and with no speed limitation, motorists had the opportunity to 'do a ton' assuming their cars where up to it[118]. Later, construction of the M6 and M5 were even closer to the estate. Concerns over the destruction of countryside

---

118 The requirement for an MOT test for cars over ten years old was introduced in 1960. The 70mph speed limit was introduced in 1965 and the breathalyser in 1967.

and communities by these wonder highways were not very vocal. In addition, the dangers of carbon dioxide emissions never seriously emerged as a topic of consideration.

Today's society is increasingly sensitive to environmental issues associated with personal car ownership. A link between gas-guzzling monsters and changes to the earth's atmosphere, including the greenhouse gas effect, has now been made. There is also acceptance of a collective guilt for societal habits like motoring and the hurt to the planet we inhabit and rely on for life. We may not be as proactive as we might in combatting and reducing environmental damage but at least these issues are on the agenda. Government's encouragement of electric or hybrid vehicles may be late, but at least it is something.

Guilt can either be shared (as with environmental damage), or it can be personal. Personal, individual guilt can prove painful and persistent, as I discovered one day down the street. It was just down from Alan's house where there was an incident that nagged at my conscience for years. The haunting event happened outside the home of a couple who had a baby that always seemed to be grizzling. The couple cared little for their appearance. All three family members were oversized and seemed to be bulging and popping out of their clothes when they moved. If I had been told that they attached tight elastic bands around their wrists and ankles, I would not have been surprised. The baby's mother had a distracted look, a ruddy complexion and untidy hair.

This particular day, the baby was unusually quiet, and was dozing in a pram outside their front door in the bright autumn sunshine. The car was nearby at the front of the driveway. Unusually, I walked alone towards the Common, and as I did, I noticed the mother taking advantage of the time available while the baby slept. She was carrying a bucket of soapy water with a yellow sponge floating on the top. She peered into the pram before turning towards the car. Then it happened. She began washing the car.

When something either wonderful or truly awful happens, it is a very human thing to stare. You cannot help yourself, something inside you seems to take control. On this occasion I am not sure quite what I was witnessing, but it was powerful. It was as if my feet had been nailed to the spot, I was transfixed by the scene unfolding in front of me. As the lady bent over to wash the car, I could see all the way up the back of her skirt. I could see her stocking tops and above that rolls of white flesh, lots of it, all the way up to the elastic on her knickers. It was like watching an accident happening and I was unable to divert my gaze. I kept on watching. What was I doing? What was I seeing? Why couldn't I move? Why was this so shockingly awful and unsexy? She was oblivious to my presence, but I wondered if anyone else had seen me do this terrible thing. After what seemed forever, I was able to make my feet move again. Turning around, I never made it to the Common, instead I walked quietly home.

Repeatedly, I replayed the incident in my mind. Each time it was more gruesome and unappealing, and I kept on feeling guilt and shame. I had at this point an undeveloped and immature understanding of God. To me, God seemed to flipflop between some benign Santa Claus and a supreme judgemental avenger. This was undoubtedly shaped by my memory of bible stories, with the second more uncomfortable image drawn from the Old Testament. I feared a formidable God of judgement capable of disapproval and revenge. Had I committed a mortal sin? Was I a pervert? God knows everything, and he knows exactly what I had done and what I had seen.

John Donne was a Jacobite poet and thinker. His most celebrated poem is 'a hymn to God the Father', which deals with the terror of death, the weight of sin and the fearful prospect of divine judgement. The poem could have been written for how I was feeling. If God disapproved, then I had blotted my mortal copy book. Then there was Mom, if ever she got wind of the incident, then goodness knows what the outcome would be. Mom could demonstrate her disapproval with more than words alone. I knew from bitter experience that her silences, disappointed glances, and general demeanour could be energy draining and leave little alternative than to reflect on what I had done to displease her.

As I returned home that day, it was no prodigal's return. The prodigal son was warmly greeted by his father. He had a party with his friends and a fine beef roast to look forward to. There was no special attention paid to my return. I knew that a fatted calf would not be on the evening menu, but a family meal of liver and dumplings followed by hot banana bake pudding was more likely. Nothing out of the ordinary, the normal modest, hot, filling meal. I sat at the table and pondered questions like, what had I done? And would my fellow diners ever find out about my dirty secret?

The whole incident left me with an unconfessed sin, worse still I might even be brought to account one day. I could not decide what was worse: the guilt, the shame, or the ultimate punishment, whatever that might be. Was I a guilty innocent?[119] All I knew for certain was that it all happened down the street.

---

119 A phrase I have borrowed from a prayer by the nineteenth century author Robert Louis Stevenson.

# Chapter Twenty

## *Swords, spirograph and sex*

Mom used to have a pad of notelets that contained the legend 'the pen is mightier than the sword' at the top of each sheet. The phrase captures a timeless truth. Throughout history, the influence of certain writers on society's attitudes and behaviour has been more potent than threats and violence. The sixties were a time of great questioning and changed attitudes, with the literature of the period providing the impetus. Famously, Harper Lee's novel *To Kill a Mockingbird* highlighted the lack of justice faced by black people in America's deep south and so highlighted the absurdity of racial discrimination more generally. Meanwhile, in Britain it was the 'angry young men' novelists and playwrights who challenged the establishment and the supremacy of the ruling classes, so spawning a vision of a meritocracy. The movement, which had begun in the previous decade, led to further publications and films based on plays and books, which attracted the phrase 'kitchen sink dramas'. In this context, the work of Kingsley Amis (*Lucky Jim*), John Braine (*Room at the Top*), John Osborne (*Look Back in Anger*) and Keith Waterhouse (*Billy Liar*) were of significance. Strangely, a woman, Shelagh Delaney, is included in the group of angry young men for writing the stage play and then co-writing the 1961 film *A Taste of Honey*. Set in the north of England, a gritty storyline tells of teenage pregnancy, rejection, a one-night stand and a union between a young white girl and a black sailor, and if that was not enough, a supportive gay man emerges as something of a hero. This play was quite unlike any other because of the way it directly challenged pre-existing norms and taboos. The small screen also played a significant role in appealing to the viewers' conscience when BBC 1 aired the drama *Cathy Come Home* in 1966. Written by Jeremy Sandford and directed by Ken Loach a truly harrowing story told of a couple struggling with homelessness, eviction and keeping their young family together. The national tenants' rights and homelessness charities *Shelter* and *Crisis*, both founded shortly after the programme, could not have dreamt of more effective publicity for their causes.

A Bob Dylan lyric of the period 'the times they are a changing' could not have been more apt, and there was good reason that the decade became tagged as 'the swinging sixties'. The sexual revolution of the time led to a wider questioning of ideas on sexual morality. In doing so, social norms defended by the family, the church and society more generally were under threat. The availability of the female contraceptive pill may have helped fuel the revolution, but the literature of the period acknowledged and possibly encouraged it. An unexpurgated edition of DH Lawrence's novel *Lady Chatterley's Lover* was first published openly in 1960. The book was the subject of much publicity and legal proceedings before it was judged not to be obscene. Having won the case, the publisher, Penguin Books, went on to sell three million copies in the next three months. Encouraged by the victory in the courts, copies of the *Kama Sutra* hit the bookstores in 1962. First translated into English in 1883, fear of Britain's obscenity laws prevented the general release of this study of society and sexuality in India 2,000 years ago. The following year the publication of *The Perfumed Garden* represented another culture's take on sex[120].

For my part, I was grateful to receive my normal Christmas present from Nan and Grandad of the *International Book of Football*. This book contained black and white action shots and interviews with mysterious players who represented teams with exotic names. I would read and re-read their stories, conjuring images of football played on a Milan training ground, the streets of Rio de Janeiro or behind the Iron Curtain. One year I had a present that out

---

120 Fifteenth-century Arabic since you ask.

trumped the *International Book of Football* in terms of stretching my imagination. A brand-new toy was on the market, the *Spirograph*, and I was fortunate enough to own one. *Spirograph* was a creative activity that involved locating coloured pens in different-sized plastic wheels and running them around a toothed ring. The ring was pinned to a piece of paper upon which satisfyingly intricate coloured patterns and shapes would emerge. You had control of the ring size and choice of colour, but the rest was beyond you. Here was a box of shapes that offered creative possibilities through a combination of art, random choice, and mathematical precision. The *Spirograph* got lots of use in our house.

One particular day, Mom called me through to the kitchen midway through creating a spiderweb type shape. I noticed that she had taken me on one side, very deliberately away from my younger brother Tim, who was engaged in building something with *Lego* bricks in the lounge.

I was furtively handed a book still cocooned in a brown paper bag. Dropping her voice, Mom told me she had bought it for me from *WH Smiths* the last time she was in Walsall. This was very strange. I knew the routine with books. You borrowed books from the school library and the 'real' library on the estate. This involved date stamping a card in the front of the book with smudgy ink and then returning it sometime later. Then there was church prize giving where you were rewarded with a book for your year's Sunday School attendance. Lastly, there was Christmas, where you might get a couple of books as presents. This book did not fit any pattern I had previously known. I was initially curious. Was it another football annual? Had I done something exceptionally good that I had forgotten all about, and was this a reward?

I pulled the book out of the bag. To my disappointment the cover was an uninspiring buff colour, bearing charcoal sketches of two children's faces. '*Peter and Pamela grow up*' was a book with dense text and a few medical-style pen and ink drawings of what looked like people's insides. (The illustrator had imagined a body spliced down the middle, in the style of the *Eagle* comic illustrations. The difference was that the *Eagle* pictures were detailed and interesting. This looked boring and complicated.)

I did my best to look appreciative. 'Thanks Mom. What's this for?'

'Well, you are getting older now and your body will be changing soon. I want you to behave like a gentleman when you grow up. The Pittaway twins' mom bought them this book, and I thought you would like a copy as well.'

I was completely baffled. Was my body changing? Changing into what? Gentlemen? Did I know any, or did she mean men in general? What bits of my behaviour did I need to worry about to be a gentleman, and how would a book on people's insides help me?

I did not understand what Mom was driving at or how the book fitted in. Sex education was not on the school curriculum and such matters were off the agenda in discussions around the family dinner table. This little book was doubtlessly well-intentioned but really was an apology for a parent/child 'facts of life' chat. Mom was raising a taboo subject, and I did not spot what was going on. I suppose I should have asked questions, but I could not think of any. Now I was embarrassed for no good reason and just wanted to get back to the *Spirograph* as quickly as I could.

As I put the book on one side, Mom looked relieved to have discharged her duty. Dad was nowhere to be seen. Tim was finishing off a *Lego* car-shaped model, and I was the owner of an unwanted gift. I never read that book even though the twins later confirmed that they had. They chose not to elaborate any further on what they made of the book.

Like most parents, Mom and Dad did not use the word 'penis'. What was strange was that they preferred using the word 'pigeon' as a substitute, as in 'when you have a bath, make sure you wash your pigeon properly'. Inevitably, schoolboys compare notes on such things, and no one else seemed to be using the word 'pigeon' in this way, apart from Tim. Pigeons, with their poor reputation as 'vermin of the air' and their grey colouring, were a curious choice as an alternative name in any case. The word also carried with it an ability to conjure strange mental images when it was used in an innocent way. The word seemed to crop up in conversations and news reports with surprising frequency. Racing pigeons, homing pigeons, pigeons descending on Trafalgar Square, and pigeon poo on the clean washing conjured hilarious images. The problem was that I was unable to share the joke with anyone else except for Tim.

I never saw either parent naked. My main reference for a woman's anatomy was the overpowering Birmingham Art Gallery experience. As this was art, looking at these paintings was not a dirty 'peeping Tom' activity. There was a plentiful supply of 'bosom' paintings on display, but beyond that nothing more. Something, perhaps a bit of cloth, a fig leaf, or a hand would be obscuring the more intimate parts of the woman's body. Nudity was never shown on the television, so apart from glances at the calendars in the barber's shop and the unfortunate encounter with Mrs Screen's knickers, this was as far as my knowledge extended. Starved of alternative reference points, I continued to believe that a woman had a pigeon. I was unsure but unconcerned as to how the physical union of a man and woman might take place and how a woman might become pregnant. In summary, I lacked common sense and curiosity in equal measure. Such matters were not of pressing interest to me. Besides, I was more interested in football.

If sex education information was in short supply, other gems of wisdom were plentiful. I was drip fed certain inescapable, indisputable truths. They may not have had the ring that 'the pen is mightier than the sword', but they were memorable none the less. Some came with grave warnings of dire consequences in cases of noncompliance.

'Be careful of swans, their wings can break your arm.'

'Don't wear someone's hat otherwise you will get nits.'

'Eat your greens or else you will get spots.'

'Wash your hands after you have been to the toilet or else you will be ill.'

'Don't wave a stick about otherwise you will have someone's eye out.'

'Don't sit on cold paving slabs or you will get piles.'

'Don't pick dandelions or you will wet your bed.'

So, it went on.

I washed my hands as instructed, but often never used soap because I never liked the feel of it. I avoided hat sharing but also shunned eating any vegetables or salad, anything green indeed. To this day I have never eaten anything green. Facial spots, even later in life as a teenager, did not distinguish me as a salad dodger. I have never met another living soul who has sustained any kind of fracture from a swan. The possibility of encountering a swan on the Yew Tree estate was minuscule in any case. During the unfortunate times in my life when I have sat waiting in Accident and Emergency hospital waiting rooms, I have never observed anyone who had lost their eye from reckless stick waving. Swan-induced injuries? A lie. Hat sharing infestations? A lie. Spot avoidance through eating vegetables? A lie. Paving slabs, lie, dandelions, lie. Lies, lies, all lies.

Away from the estate, significant societal change was happening, and long-established norms were being openly challenged. For my part, I tried to follow the broad outlines of what Mom and Dad said, even if I drew the line at eating greens. In terms of the gift I had been given that day, Peter and Pamela could not compete with the *Spirograph* or the *International Book of Football* in firing my imagination.

# Chapter Twenty-one

## *A very significant year*

There is something about the year 1966. For those wishing to put the Gregorian calendar on one side in favour of dividing the population by age, it is a big year. It represents the artificial line between those born after the war (the so-called 'baby boomers') and younger groups who follow[121]. For others who witnessed one key event, however, the year assumes an even greater significance. My country cannot credibly claim world supremacy in many things. There was however one glorious exception, which occurred one sunny afternoon in July 1966. That 'thing' took on undue significance for me and meant that for four years England were undisputed world football champions.

In terms of the 'where were you when …?' question, I have vivid memories of England's once-in-a-lifetime triumph[122]. I experienced the excitement through the tiny television screen in the corner of the family front room. In the sixties, live televised football was normally restricted to one game a year – the FA Cup final; 1966 was different. For a golden period of two and a half weeks, the World Cup tournament came 'home'. I watched just about every England game live and kept a scrap book of newspaper and magazine cuttings.

During the six months before the competition, the World Cup was kept firmly on everyone's radar by constant media coverage. The Post Office even issued stamps depicting images of footballers. Then there was a strange character whose presence

---

121 Firstly, generation x, then generation y, millennials, and now generation z.

122 At the time of writing the achievement of being crowned world champions has not been repeated. I sincerely hope this footnote now looks dated.

was hard to ignore. The creature in question was the official World Cup mascot, a strange cartoon/teddy bear style lion who was humanised by walking on his rear legs and wearing a suit compete with a union flag waistcoat. When not appearing on TV or in newspapers, Willie cropped up on a range of products. The following rather formal advertisement (which appeared in the January 1966 edition of *Charles Buchan's Football Monthly* magazine) is not untypical:

'The official World Cup Willie tie, club quality 15/6d. Lillywhites are proud to announce that we have been granted the exclusive licence by the Football Association for the World Cup Willie Tie, all soccer enthusiasts will want to show their support for this outstanding festival of football.'

For my part, I owned a World Cup Willie white plastic football. By the time the competition began, Willie's image had worn off the ball following merciless kicking on all sorts of unsuitable surfaces. What had not worn off was the nation's appetite for the competition and my enthusiasm to see England play.

Thanks to the technology of the time, I can say that I witnessed the monumental achievement of taking on the world and emerging as champions, all from the lounge/sitting room of 26 Lilac Avenue. Most families I knew owned or rented a television set. There were two distinct approaches to acknowledging its presence in the front room. The first involved disguising the set as just another piece of household furniture. That meant enclosing the set in a polished wooden box meant to look like a drinks cabinet, or something similar. The second approach was to celebrate a pinnacle of technological achievement by putting the set on legs and adding a lower shelf, which was just right for keeping a current copy of the *Radio Times* handy. (Most TV viewing of the period was pre-planned by reference to the printed listings in the *Radio Times*. Although the weekly publication contained details of all BBC TV and radio listings, it did not contain ITV listings.) We opted for the second approach, with the set standing uncertainly on legs with a flat wood effect top wide enough to accommodate a mobile aerial and lamp.

There is a certain iconic image of a fair-haired Bobby Moore, England's captain, holding the golden trophy high against a clear blue sky. He is supported on the shoulders of sweat-stained teammates. My memory is of seeing this and being caught up in the atmosphere and colour of it all: the orange-brown ball, the distinctive red England football shirts and the many flags waved in the crowd. My memory however is faulty. This is not what I witnessed. The match was transmitted in black and white[123]. Most clips of the match appearing on *YouTube* and the like are from a full length, colour feature film called *Goal* that was made to record the tournament. In those days all televised images were grainy and viewed through nineteen-inch screens, which is only slightly bigger than my laptop screen.

A record home TV audience of over thirty-two million people watched the final. This is a staggering figure considering that fifteen years earlier TV ownership was quite rare. In terms of sales of TV sets, the coronation of Queen Elizabeth II in 1953 was a game changer. Ownership doubled between 1952 and 1954. By the time of her coronation, despite the boost in sales, there were only 3.25 million sets across the country. Many who were unable to stump up £70 (nearly two months' wages) crammed into more fortunate neighbours' houses for the occasion. They were rewarded with a flickering black-and-white image broadcast on a single channel. By 1966 the lower relative price of a set and availability of rental meant that many more families had access to the momentous event. Television viewing choice had also expanded to three channels: BBC, ITV and BBC2. BBC later became BBC1 and was seen as the 'official' channel. ITV, by comparison, was a bit of a guilty pleasure being unashamedly commercial and lacking the gravitas of the BBC. A bit flashy, in fact, and therefore something to be treated with some suspicion. The curious and over serious BBC2 was the newcomer,

---

123 The BBC did not announce that they would be transmitting programmes in colour until a year later.

being introduced in 1964. This new-fangled channel required a certain type of TV set, or aerial, or both. Mr Houghton, who lived just around the corner, claimed to have picked up the new channel by shoving a knitting needle into the back of his set. Most families used the more conventional route of upgrading their rented set for a few shillings more per week. I have a friend called Tony who recalls growing up with a rented TV in the house with a difference. The set was 'pay as you go' and operated by a coin-fed meter – a device to help those who knew that they would have problems budgeting. The collector from the rental company would arrive every month or so, count the takings in the coin meter and deduct and retain the rental charge. Happily, the reckoning up normally resulted in a small pile of excess coins being placed on top of the TV. The family were then able to watch something 'for free'. This gave the opportunity for random and casual television watching rather than the normal purposeful viewing routine.

Back to the year in question and preparations for welcoming the finest international sides on the globe were being finalised. The technology was in place (well, our TV set worked). Willie, despite his lack of facial expression, seemed expectant, and so was I. This just had to be a tournament like no other. Happily, record books show that a dream outcome resulted on 30 July 1966 when England won the trophy. Yet the dream nearly became a nightmare. England had lost the World Cup before they won it – literally.

The fiasco of the missing Cup took place on 20 March and came about following a decision to display the (Jules Rimet) trophy in the build-up to the competition. Bizarrely, the trophy was to be on show as part of a postage stamp exhibition, of all things, at Westminster's Central Hall, London, of all places. The Cup was housed behind a simple display cabinet, and two security guards, one an old age pensioner, were given the job of keeping an eye on things. When they both enjoyed a tea break together in another room, thieves let themselves in through an emergency exit and simply walked out with the twelve-inch trophy. To say it did not take a master criminal to pull off the heist would not be overstating things. Scotland Yard took control of the criminal investigation but could not make a breakthrough until a ransom note for £15,000 was received. (To add some perspective, the average house price was a little over £2,000 at the time.) This led to finding and arresting one of the thieves. Unfortunately, the thief was not cooperating and was not letting on where the trophy was or if indeed it had been melted down for its gold value. The intense scrutiny of the entire world was clearly on The English Football Association (FA). They were responsible; the trophy was missing, and the clock was ticking down until the start of the competition.

This was a time well before the invention of cell phones; indeed, most homes could not afford a landline. Anyone wanting to make a telephone call would have to take a pocket full of change to the nearest red public telephone box[124]. So, Dave Corbett left his home in Norwood, South London to make a phone call, taking his collie dog, Pickles, with him. On the way, the dog had to do what dogs do best in some bushes and discovered the trophy encased in newspaper and bound with string.

The FA, FIFA (the world's football governing body) and the country breathed a collective sigh of relief. Pickles' life changed forever, and the dog became an overnight celebrity. Pickles received numerous awards, including one from the National Canine Defence League, won Dog of the Year and appeared on television, including the children's programmes *Blue Peter* and *Magpie*, as well as featuring in a film[125].

With a trophy in place for the victors to raise, preparations were well advanced. England's manager, Alf Ramsey, was an abrupt, single-minded sort with a quirky faux upper-class accent

---

124 There was a blue equivalent used by the police. This is featured in the long running television show Dr Who as the famed Tardis.

125 Called *The Spy with a Cold Nose* since you ask.

and a clear plan. Ramsey took his playing squad to live and train at the FA's headquarters at Lilleshall, Shropshire, away from their wives and families. Here, for a full two months, he inflicted a military-style regime designed to foster camaraderie and teamwork.

Ticket sales at venues such as Villa Park, Birmingham, and Goodison Park Liverpool, gave supporters an opportunity to see for themselves great players such as Lev Yashin, Pele and Eusebio. Then there were teams like the current world campions, Brazil, the technical Italians, the sinister USSR and the mysterious North Koreans[126] to see. The entire nation could also follow the unusually extensive coverage on TV, radio and the back pages of all the newspapers.

Conveniently, England somehow managed to arrange for all their games to be played at the national stadium, Wembley. After an unconvincing start to the competition, they stumbled through the group and early knockout stages to face Portugal in the semi-final. Mr Skinner from next door but one said that if we were to win, we would go on to win the tournament. England won 2-1 and all was set for the final. I could not conceive of any other outcome than an England triumph. When it came to football, Mr Skinner knew what he was talking about. England's opponents in the final were West Germany. The legacy of defeat in the Second World War left Germany partitioned on ideological grounds, with East Germany being communist-controlled. West Germany remained a democracy. The need for a physical border to separate one country from another is somehow a little sad; when a physical border separates a country from itself, as was the case with Germany, it seems far worse[127].

In the final, a noisy Wembley crowd of 96,924 and a huge TV audience witnessed poor defending by both sides, which made for

---

126 Quirkily North Korea was recognised by FIFA as a country but not the United Nations.

127 Germany was reunified in 1990.

an exciting, goal-laden affair. The match went into extra time after the Germans scored late on to make the score 2-2. England's key third goal that put them ahead was controversial, to say the least. (This was a time a million years before goal-line technology, VAR, or indeed different camera angles.) For the viewer at home there was no such thing as action replays, let alone slow-motion replays. You saw the incident once in real time, and that was it. It is worth mentioning at this point that the referee and the linesman[128] at the centre of the incident looked as if they had accessorised their normal day clothes with a pair of shorts and were reluctantly helping at an inter-school match because the real officials had failed to turn up. Against a backdrop of baying England supporters, the two men held a 'did it cross the line?' discussion for what seemed an eternity. Mr Bahramov the Russian linesman, was one of the very few people who felt he had seen the ball cross the line. Goal! The Germans were still smarting over the decision when Geoff Hurst on a breakaway added his third and England's fourth and final goal in the dying seconds of the game. There were wild celebrations in the stadium and in homes up and down the country. Looking back on the event, I am struck by the fact that union flags, and not crosses of St. George, were waved enthusiastically in the stadium in celebration. All that mattered was that England had won, and BBC commentator Kenneth Wolstenholme confirmed as much. Wolstenholme was an old school broadcaster who provided the much-repeated soundtrack to the dying seconds of the game by uttering, 'There are people on the pitch ... they think it is all over ... it is now'. Few would remember any phrases poor Hugh Johns provided on the rival channel's commentary (identical pictures were transmitted live on both BBC and ITV).

After seeing Bobby Moore collect the trophy from the Queen, Dad started to get the tea together. Mom did not see the match

---

128 Now ludicrously called an assistant referee.

with us because she had a Saturday job at Pimm's hardware store at the bottom of Lilac Avenue. Dad agreed to let me go and tell her the good news. As I excitedly ran down the street, something was very different. I was perfectly alone in the street. There was no one to be seen. Absolutely no one. No one outside, no one in cars. I could not even hear any cars in neighbouring streets. It was eerily quiet, and this was a hot July afternoon. Had the Russians 'dropped the bomb'? Was this why Mr Bahramovwas so distracted earlier? Was this the end of the world? Or was it simply the case that everyone was indoors watching the celebrations after the match? Arriving at the normally busy shop, I found that it was totally devoid of customers. There were just two shop assistants there, Mom and another lady. They were listening to the unfolding celebrations on Wembley's pitch on a portable radio and seemed very happy. Two women with little or no interest in football listening to a live commentary? Deserted shops and empty streets? Strange days indeed. Yew Tree estate had caught football fever.

Next morning, our family got up to experience the normal Sunday routine of church and roast dinner. The eleven England heroes picked up their £60 appearance money, doubtless nursing hangovers and awaited a £1,000 bonus for winning the competition. England were world champions.

Given this country's excellent transport and infrastructure coupled with state-of-the-art stadia, it is perhaps curious that the competition has never been staged on English soil since this time. This is especially so when venues such as South Korea, Japan, and even the State of Qatar have been favoured despite lacking pre-existing facilities and having no football history to speak of.

The answer may lie in the ineptitude displayed by the FA. If losing the trophy was not enough, the victory celebrations were completely mishandled. Players had not seen their wives for two months. Now the tournament was over, players could meet with their loved ones and relish the moment. The bad news was that the FA had organised a dinner at a top London hotel. Wives were briefly reunited with their footballing partners before putting on their glad rags for a very special meal. Unfortunately, the wives were not invited. There was not enough room for them as well as the FA great and good and various hangers on. Instead, they were shunted into a side room for the evening. To say they were furious was an understatement. One can only speculate that there may even have been violence inflicted on World Cup Willie and members of the FA had they realised at the time that somehow spare places had been found for Pickles the dog and his owner!

Football in 1966 was very different from the game it is today. One major difference was that there were no substitutes allowed. The manager picked eleven players to see the game through, and if there were injuries or players not performing, so be it. As a result, the final was watched by squad members not making the final cut and having no chance to participate in the biggest game they would ever be associated with. So, an unfortunate Jimmy Greaves, England's star striker going into the tournament, would observe his replacement Geoff Hurst make history by scoring a hat trick[129]. From then on, the eleven players selected in the final would forever be introduced with the preface 'World Cup winner ...' Only eleven Englishmen have had such a distinction. (By comparison there have been twelve Americans who have walked on the moon's surface.) The eleven men making the final became national heroes, constantly appearing on TV, in newspapers and when their playing careers ended at sportsman's dinners for years to come.

One remarkable fact is that two of the eleven players came from one family, the Charlton brothers. Facially they looked alike, but that is where the similarity ended. Older brother Jack was a tall, tough centre half who could head a ball further than most

---

129 Hurst's achievement was matched in the 2022 World Cup Final by France's Kylian Mbappe. His side did not raise the trophy however being beaten on penalties by Argentina.

people could kick. He resembled how a Disney cartoon would depict a loping giraffe on speed. Bobby, by comparison, hardly ever headed the ball. He was however a graceful player who, like a bee, buzzed purposefully across the grass in a gliding motion. His biggest asset was that he possessed a stinging shot, which he often employed anywhere within thirty yards of the goal. The victorious eleven were a potent mixture of artists and artisans who had been skilfully blended by manager Alf Ramsey, a man knighted for his efforts. There were villains in their ranks, such as Nobby Stiles, who attempted to decapitate a French player earlier in the competition (so reducing the opposition to ten men) and 'hard as nails' Jackie Charlton. There were the hard workers such as Peters, Ball and Hunt. Then there were the cultured players in the form of Bobby Charlton and Bobby Moore. It is a cruel irony that at least half of the victorious team that day contracted dementia in later life. Those who created unforgettable memories were themselves deprived of any memory of the event.

The week after the World Cup victory, a breathless school friend, Ian Houghton, called by. He was going to Delves Post Office to get the 'new' stamps before they sold out, and did I want to do the same? The Post Office had taken one of the football themed stamps and put on a limited run with the words 'ENGLAND WINNERS' printed on it in recognition of the monumental achievement. He said they were going to be valuable one day. I told Mom, but she said they would not be worth anything. I later wished I had gone with Ian and blown what pocket money I had on these 4d. (2 pence) perforated mementoes, whether they would become valuable or not.

The impact of the World Cup victory was great. Football league attendances rose by one million the following season, and something significant happened to me. As I pasted pictures cut from newspapers of Bobby Moore and Bobby Charlton into my scrapbook, a profound thought occurred. I realised that no footballers were called Robert. I needed to change my name. I decided there and then to rename myself Bob and practiced my autograph over and over for when I became a footballer. I never became a footballer. I did however become Bob, seizing the opportunity of a senior school to rebrand myself. Today no one except for my brother Tim knows me as Robert.

The highpoint of 1966 was seen by a British record television audience. The black and white coverage seemed inappropriate for celebrating the sunshine, mood, colour, and exuberance of the occasion. The black and white images, however, were entirely appropriate when bringing news of the low point of the same year a few months later. The lack of colour somehow helped convey the dirt, despair, and disaster of a truly awful tragedy.

It took just five minutes for one of the National Coal Board's slag heaps to slide down the rain-soaked mountain overlooking Aberfan, South Wales. The rushing landslide of coal waste, mud and debris engulfed a farm, several houses and the village junior school beginning its first lesson of the day. The awful sight, along with news of failed rescue efforts, absorbed most of the news coverage for several weeks. The disaster left a community stunned and helpless and exacted a terrible death toll of 116 children and 28 adults. The pathetic images of bodies being dug out of the filth days after the landslide and reports of a mass funeral for the victims in the weeks after the disaster were overpowering. Like the rest of the country, I looked on with my parents at the shocking images.

Regrettably, not a week goes by without some bad news story hitting the headlines. Some tragedies seem too great or distant to fully understand. You just absorb the information and feel sorry for the human suffering and cost of life. Aberfan was different. The village is closer to the Yew Tree Estate than London. The events seemed to be so awful because they were easy to relate to. I knew what a British primary school was like: the desks, the scaled-down chairs, the plant monitors, the milk crates and the pegs for coats and bags. I saw the news programmes and heard survivors of a devastated community with a population less than half the size of the Yew Tree Estate trying to come to terms with the brutality of it all. Grieving parents were the same age as people who stood at my school gate.

I have strong memories of this particular year. The year was of a single glorious searing achievement and one incident of unimaginable awfulness.

# Chapter Twenty-two

## *Everlasting Love*

It happened unexpectedly one Saturday morning in 1966. Undoubtedly under the influence of post-World Cup euphoria, and only too aware of my obsession with the beautiful game, Dad announced that he was going to take me to a 'real' match. It was too cold for Tim, anyway he was too young, so it was just the two of us. I was, as they are alleged to say in the business, 'over the moon' by this unexpected offer that also promised a rare father/son bonding opportunity.

Looking at the fixture listings in the newspaper, Dad reviewed the possibilities.

'Albion? Could be crowded and difficult to park. Wolves? Away from home today. Walsall? Why not? It's an FA Cup match, it could be good. Let's watch the saddlers'

'Who are Walsall playing, Dad? ... Who? ... Saint who?'

St. Neots Town conjured up a place in a long-lost land of knights and dragons. Who would name their town after a saint no one had heard of? This could be a strange affair.

'Where is St. Neots, Dad?'

Judging by his evasive answers, Dad was as well informed as I was. Not that it mattered. I was off to see a real match.

After a quick lunch and setting out in good time, we passed the Common into the Delves area of Walsall and, taking in the route by the sewerage works, Dad found a place to park the car. Joining other groups of people heading in the same direction, we marched towards where the match was to be played. The floodlights pinpointed the exact location of Fellows Park, a ground named after a previous Chairman with more money than sense who had single-handedly kept the club financially afloat. Sitting snuggly alongside a railway line, the ground was next to a road bridge that offered views of half the pitch for those unwilling to pay the admission price and put up with watching at a considerable distance.

The whole area buzzed with life. There was a faint smell of onions and hot dogs, and plenty of people milling about the Wallows Lane entrance. Someone was selling rosettes and club badges from a pinboard, and an old man advertised copies of Saturday's *Express and Star* lunchtime edition by holding a copy high in one hand. Vendors yelled the price of match programmes and were rewarded by a brisk trade from those prepared to part with a silver shilling piece[130] to see the editor's stab at what the team line ups might be.

Arriving at the turnstiles, I waited my turn in the juniors' queue and passed over the coins Dad had given me. Pushing my middle region against the ice-cold metal of the contraption there was a clunk, and I was inside the ground. Dad followed through one of the adjacent turnstiles.

I had entered a strange and wonderful place well in advance of the 3p.m. kick-off. The ground could have been taken from a doodle in Heath Robinson's sketchbook. It was a concrete and corrugated steel concoction that had evolved over many decades, and unashamedly reflected a 'make do and mend' philosophy. It was not unlike all stadia of its time[131], just a bit quirkier than

---

130  Now 5p which is worth 75p today.
131  The time predated the awful disasters resulting in loss of life at Heysel, Bradford, and Hillsborough by some twenty years and the impetus for a ground rebuilding programme aimed at safety and comfort.

most. Four floodlight pylons of different sizes stood in each corner, representing relatively recent additions[132]. The fact that the ground had four sides of terracing at all was also a recent improvement with the demolition of Orgill's laundry wall behind the railway end goal a few seasons earlier.

As I made my way through people standing around, my sense of smell was attacked by a combination of *Bovril* beef drink, *Brylcreem* hair cream and body odours. We entered an uncovered, narrow terrace that had been crowbarred in where the laundry wall had once stood. In front of us, a shallow wall guarded a shale running track, a set of goalposts and the playing area beyond, which had a noticeable corner-to-corner slope. The pitch itself was a combination of lush grass and mud and sand around the centre circle and the penalty areas.

There was some roof cover to the end opposite us at Hillary Street and the terrace to the right. This comprised a patchwork of part rusting and, when it rained, sometimes leaky roofing materials. Each of the four terraces around the pitch were different sizes and inclines. The cinder bank at the far Hilary Street end sloped viciously towards the corner flag. From this corner, teams appeared from the dressing room and disappeared again at half and full time. It was behind this terrace that the toilet facilities were situated, these involved descending a hundred feet or so and urinating on corrugated steel sheets into a drain while staring at a railway line below. The right-hand terrace was deeper and more even. Straddling the halfway line on the left-hand side was a modest stand. Here a few hundred people paid a few pence more for the privilege of squeezing into wooden seats. The rest of us found a crush barrier to lean against or a piece of concrete slab to share with others for the next few hours.

---

132 Walsall's floodlights were first introduced in late 1957.

Some starry-eyed writers have likened football stadia to cathedrals for the masses. Fellows Park was nothing of the sort. It was more a tin chapel for believers and the cynical who wanted to believe. More accurately, it resembled several tin chapels spot riveted together by an inebriated welder with poor eyesight and a good sense of humour. This had been the home of Walsall, the Saddlers, for the past seventy years and was now a glorious crumbling wreck. I was fascinated by the quirkiness of it all.

Children chattered, ate sweets, and sang strange songs as the time ticked away towards the big kick-off. They crowded together at the front of the terrace, some in red and white scarves and others in red and white woollen hats. In these pre-merchandise days, these were doubtless knitted by thoughtful family members. There were also a number holding wooden rattles decorated in club colours. Some rattles were obviously homemade, possibly as part of school woodwork lessons, others were bought as Government surplus stock. (Government standard rattles were originally used in wartime to warn of a gas attack and the need to put masks on.) I looked on with envy at a few children who had the full complement of scarf, hat, rosette, and rattle.

Men smoked and talked about all things football and some things not. Some produced foil-wrapped sandwiches from their coat pockets, which they devoured greedily. There were a lot of in-jokes and mild swearing. Some men were still wearing boiler suits and work clothes and had obviously travelled directly from a factory to join their mates at the game. Judging by the smell of beer breath, some had also taken a detour to a pub. Teenage boys with their ubiquitous cigarettes were laughing and joking and trying to look 'cool'.

I immediately loved this place, and I was fascinated by its atmosphere. I had never experienced anything like it before. Dad had brought me to a place steeped in history, and I was about to see a little piece of history take place. In the early days of organised football and following the success of the twelve clubs forming a Football League in 1888, a second division was created four years later, including Walsall[133]. Founded in 1888, the club predated others who have since become global brands like Liverpool, Chelsea, and Manchester City. Strangely, little St. Neots Town had an even longer history than Walsall, being formed in 1879. I was about to see two well-established teams competing in the world's oldest, most famous and glamorous cup competition.

This was the biggest game in St. Neots Town's history. A large noisy away following had made their way from West Cambridgeshire to the Black Country for the occasion, swelling the gate to double its normal size. Hopes of a giant-killing were quashed as the home side huffed and puffed, missed a penalty, and eventually ran out winners with two late goals.

After my first experience of seeing Walsall play, I wanted more. I thought it was great, I had caught the bug. From that point onwards I returned many times, long after Dad had regained his senses and lost interest completely.

My first trip to Fellows Park to see an evening kick-off was an unexpectedly vibrant affair. The floodlights ensured the match was played in glorious Technicolor. The white shirts and red shorts of the players glowed, and the grass took on a different form, like a fully lit snooker table in a dark room. Standing close to the touchline, I spotted details I had never noticed before, like the drops of rain resting on the surface of the pitch and the *Vaseline* jelly on the eyebrows of 'our' centre half, a player with the less than exotic name of Stan Jones.

One of the quirkier features of the game was the presence of a 'sponge man' who doubled as the team's trainer. If a player

---

133 Or Walsall Town Swifts to be more accurate.

went down injured, he would run onto the pitch from the dugout carrying a half full bucket of water and a wet sponge. The same sponge was applied to wipe blood away, revive a player by holding it to the back of their neck, or wipe dirt away from a wound. The sponge apparently had magical reviving and healing qualities.

One thing that I had not expected but soon got used to was the ritual of goalkeepers knocking imaginary mud off their boots by back kicking the goalpost before taking a goal kick. The noise of the studs on the goalframe resounded all around the stadium. The sound was familiar and welcomed from your own goalkeeper. When the opposition goalkeeper did the same thing, it was irritating and evidence of unnecessary time wasting.

When he was old enough, brother Tim joined me at the matches. We saw yeoman-like footballers with salt of the earth names like Frank, Colin, and Mick. The players for the most part were unglamorous, robust, no-nonsense types, the sort of guys who would deliver coal for you or offer to repair your drive for cash in hand. This was a couple of generations before professional footballers metamorphosed into the toned athletes they have become today.

We never sat in the stand. We always stood, often quite close to the pitch, which was great unless it rained. If it did everyone headed for the cover of a leaky roof at the back of the terrace. With no gates or fences it was possible to reposition yourself during the game, and it was not uncommon to see children stand behind one goal in the first half and then appear at the back of the opposite goal in the second half. Part of the experience meant that I could be so close to the pitch that I could hear the players call to one another. I picked up expressions such as 'man on', 'hold', 'steady' and 'look up'. I was able to use these when I played myself, so giving the illusion that I was a better player than I was.

In terms of the playing kits, teams of the era wore shirts unsullied by advertising logos and messages, the manufacturers' emblems or, indeed, the club badge. These were clean, classic club colours, which were sadly impossible to buy as replica kits. The shirts were devoid of the names of the players and double-digit squad numbers. Numbering of shirts extended from one to twelve (twelve being the newly introduced substitute role), and the match day programme identified the player wearing that shirt on a particular day. The numbering of one to eleven offered some sort of clue as to the role the player was meant to perform. All 5s operated in the middle of the defence, and all 9s acted as centre forwards; 7s and 11s were meant to offer width, while 2s and 3s defended from the touchlines, and so on. Today's footballers wear boots that look as flimsy as carpet slippers in colours such as yellow and pink. Back then all boots were sturdy and black, and the only pink colour to be found was the paper colour of the local Saturday evening *Sporting Star* and the *Sports Argus*.

Virtually every professional football game is covered live by both national and regional radio with some matches enjoying full match commentary. The era of my upbringing predated both local radio and the internet, so the luxury of this attention was absent. I was impressed and fascinated by the fact that a match could finish at 4.40pm on a Saturday and then be reported in the two local pink newspapers, which appeared as early as 5.45 pm in newsagents. (The *Sporting Star* was produced in Wolverhampton and the *Sports Argus* in Birmingham.) This was as close as it got to getting completely up-to-date news coverage. For the newspapers to achieve this impressive feat, the content not involving match reports was already typeset and printed during the week, and the outer page reports were phoned through from grounds and hurriedly made up and printed. Inevitably, the volume and detail on second half incidents were noticeably slimmer than the first fifteen minutes of the match. Rather than taking a reflective standpoint as matches are reported today, reporting involved a straightforward chronological account of significant happenings along the lines of 'in the ninth minute Taylor fired a shot wide, then in the tenth minute, Murray went close with a header from a corner taken by Morris ...' and so on.

At matches I always felt compelled to buy a match day programme despite its lack of reading content and modest production values. The *Saddlers News* consisted of sixteen pages of mainly adverts and statistics. It had the same sort of home-made feel that you might find in a programme produced for a school sports day or a country fair. Although there was no colour photography or action shots, it did contain a *Football League Review* magazine which doubled its size. Local adverts contained unlikely phone numbers and exhortations to use a Cliff football 'as used by the Saddlers' (available from Lawrence and Platers), 'follow the Saddlers every Friday in the Walsall Observer' or consider a heating system like that in the Saddlers club (which was installed by Manton Heating Limited). If you weren't excited by the prospect of a football, a weekly newspaper, or a new heating system, then there was Banister and Thatcher, a chemist a mere 200 yards from the ground or an opportunity to invest in a four per cent tax paid share account with the Walsall Mutual Building Society. Then there was the 'deliberate mistake' competition and the 'lucky programme draw'. Finally, there was an alphabetic key to the teams involved in matches elsewhere, which became relevant when half time scores were displayed against the letters A to T at two strategic points in the stadium early in the second half.

About this time, newspapers and magazines sometimes offered a gift of league ladders to readers. This consisted of a cardboard sheet featuring the division structure set out as four ladders. The ladders contained ninety-two small slits. Coloured tabs, one for each of the ninety-two clubs, made it possible to move teams up and down after a round of games was completed on a Saturday teatime. Not everyone was prepared to go to this trouble. I was for a while, but the Walsall red and white tab never seemed to move very far in either direction. Walsall never did anything spectacular, like being promoted or relegated, it just staged battles and remained resolutely mid-table in the third tier of English football. (In this less complicated era, it was known as the Third Division.)

As someone watching a third-tier side, it would be safe to assume that I had never seen my side pit their wits against the big-name players in league action. This would however be incorrect. Over the years I have seen games against an opposition that boasted players who had played at the top flight of the game, including some who were part of England's 1966 triumph. All the players involved were admittedly winding down their careers[134] when they appeared at Fellows Park. I was nevertheless privileged to see these former world champions playing against my side. It is inconceivable that any of today's top stars would ever consider playing this far down the football pyramid in their mid-thirties as these players did. Thanks to the money in the game today, most top-level footballers can expect to approach retirement as millionaires. The earning capacity of players in the sixties could not compare.

Contrary to the alleged utterance of the onetime Liverpool Manager, Bill Shankly, that football is more serious than life and death, it is not. For many, however, including myself, football is the most important of the least important things in life. My interest however is more specific. It is not so much the game itself as the team.

Do you take this team, Walsall, to be your team to have and to hold, for better, for worse, for richer, for poorer, in sickness

---

134 They were Bobby Moore (for Fulham), Bobby Charlton and Nobby Stiles (for Preston) and Alan Ball (for Blackpool).

and in health, forsaking all others, to love and to cherish until death do you part?

I do.

Since that November day in 1966 Walsall became my team. Walsall. Plain old Walsall. Other clubs have exotic-sounding names, like neighbouring clubs Albion, Wanderers and Villa. Other teams featured in the fixtures list had names like Wednesday, Hotspur, Park Avenue and Thistle. Why didn't we have a more glamorous name? When the club was founded in 1888, it involved a merger of two local sides, Walsall Town and Walsall Swifts. The club was formed as Walsall Town Swifts but dropped the more elegant appendages a little later. I used to wish that the club was still called Walsall Town Swifts[135].

Some speak of their 'happy place', somewhere that person treasures for the happy memories that can become a shelter and a comfort. Although I was constantly drawn to the same place, Fellows Park, it was never by any stretch of the imagination my happy place. I have heard it said that the game is about pleasurable and pain. My own experience has been one more of numb discomfort. Watching my team, the hours involved, the matches, season after season, year after year, never getting promoted or relegated, just pitting themselves against other teams who, for the most part, were equally inept. Both Dad and Tim continued watching Walsall for a while before concluding that this was not a healthy thing for any well-adjusted human being to do. So, I went alone for a while before forging several valued friendships with others who had the same affliction as myself.

---

135 The swift appears on the club's coat of arms. The club is not nicknamed the Swifts, instead it is the Saddlers – a recognition of one of the town's primary industries in 1888 (there were 600 leather works in Walsall at that time).

Much later, after I was married, the relegations and promotions began. I took my two sons along to see Walsall play, buying them season tickets even. They stuck with it for a few years and then spotted the futility of it all and stopped coming to matches. I suppose they grew up. I never did[136].

136 I have since taken my two grandsons to a Walsall game. Things went well and we won 3-1.

# THE BIG TIDY UP

# The big tidy up

I am blessed to have lived a full life that has included a happy childhood. The reminiscences and reflections in the previous chapters centre on my first decade of life. Inevitably much has changed since this time, and I have left several loose ends that need tidying up.

In terms of bringing things up to date, I should start with the obvious. There was no act of war involving nuclear weapons. The Soviets never took it upon themselves to bomb the estate, or the potentially messier target of the nearby sewerage works, or anywhere else in the country for that matter. The collective fear of attack, counterattack, and complete planetary annihilation was unfounded. Despite a narrow escape during the 1962 Cuban missile crisis, the nuclear Sword of Damocles never fell. For those who did not live through it, the nuclear threat might be dismissed as ridiculous paranoia. I can confirm however that the threat felt both real and close at the time. This was a truly terrifying period of history where you were brought up to fear a bogeyman who could strike at any time. Nowadays, the prospect of an environmental implosion rather than nuclear apocalypse seems more likely. Despite this, thinking and priorities have been shaped by the past to such an extent that £40 billion a year is committed to the nation's current defence budget.

The nuclear threat receded because the bogeyman himself disappeared. People power led to the fall of the Berlin Wall in late 1989. A reforming Soviet leadership declined to respond to the event. This was a truly pivotal moment in time. The breaking down of the object that physically divided a city, and metaphorically a country and a continent, was a clarion call for something even bigger. Light was now streaming through the Iron Curtain, and hard-line communism's influence on Eastern and Central Europe was fading. By 1990 the Cold War was declared over, and Germany was reunified. The following year the Soviet Union was led to a peaceful dissolution under its then President Mikhail Gorbachev. The USSR had, up until that point, existed for seventy years, the entire lifetime of both my generation and my parent's generation.

Without a bogeyman, what was the point of a Cold War? The only rational answer could be no point at all. By the 1990s common sense had broken out, and the world became a safer place as a result. Under such circumstances, issues of winners and losers might be considered a superfluous issue to ponder. American comedian and documentary maker Rich Hall did however try to do just that. After considering all the evidence he concluded that neither side won. The War was a massive stalemate. Given that the War was about each side defending an opposing philosophy, it was curious, he felt, that thirty years later there had been a 'flipping' of ideologies. The US government (then under Republican Donald Trump) ruled by lies, intimidation, and smear tactics while Russia embraced gangster capitalism to became 'a gas station with a bunch of rusty nukes out back.' (Russia being responsible then for twelve per cent of the world's oil supply).

Returning to the narrow escape of the Cuban missile crisis, few looking back could conclude that it was anything but a powder keg of a situation. It should be recalled that as part of an uneasy peace, the US placed stringent sanctions on Cuba *'(to) bring about hunger, desperation, and overthrow of the government'*. Today, Soviet support to Cuba has dried up, yet US sanctions continue against a small island that remains proudly communist. The US policy has palpably failed – the Cuban government has not been overthrown, and there is no desperation or starvation. Cuba has stood strong against the embargo, becoming even more self-sufficient after the Soviet disintegration. Communist control of the island has brought with it a well-regulated system that has proved successful. Price controls on food and state grocery stores guarantee all Cubans vital goods at affordable prices. Cuba is in fact one of the few Latin American countries to have eliminated hunger and child malnutrition. Denied the option of importing new replacement US motors, Cuba has the finest examples of operational 1950s American vehicles in the world. The resourcefulness of mechanics preserving and keeping these cars on the road without imported replacement parts is impressive. It is impossible not to admire the resilience of this tiny island nation. As a nation, the United Kingdom had to survive a world war without imported food, which was tough. Thankfully, the lack of imports lasted less than six years; Cuba by comparison has survived a US embargo for over six decades.

The word 'peace' is often abused in its usage. During my early years, the West, led by America, claimed there could be 'peace' through the concept of mutually assured destruction. To properly compete in a Cold War meant entering a nuclear arms race. Then there was the effort to convince the public of the need for the need for these actions. In Britain this involved frightening the living daylights out of the population as to the 'likely' consequences of no action. In Hebrew, the word 'shalom' provides a fuller understanding of peace encompassing mutual well-being, harmony, wholeness, and completeness. The 'peace' that respective power blocks claimed involved a demonising of the other side, repeating a convincing narrative of the need for a nuclear deterrent and massive expenditure on nuclear weapons and espionage. This may have produced peace of a sort, but it was a pale imitation of shalom. It was a phoney peace, involving a shared fear that the worst might happen at any time and a diversion of finite national resources to maintaining positions.

Growing up, I was very aware of the danger in admittedly simplistic terms. A lasting peace seemed impossible given the existence of a Soviet bogeyman, nuclear stockpiling, and the Cold War. It is a source of great encouragement that when situations seem hopeless and a breakthrough impossible, then events may turn out more positively than you dare imagine. By the early

1990s, as the obstacles to peace began to fade, I had two young children of my own. I am grateful that they did not have to spend their childhood years in the same adversarial and threatening climate that I did.

So, with a reduced nuclear threat and the Cold War outdated, life could go on as before, this time unhindered by fear. The nearby sewerage works could continue to do what it had done for a hundred years, as could Fellows Park, the home of my beloved football team. Or so I thought. Today, a *Morrisons* supermarket now occupies the site of what was Fellows Park, and the football club has a new home, on the site of the former sewerage works! The optimist in me hoped this new home could mark an upturn in playing fortunes. Little did I know that the 1086Domesday Book described the site as a 'wasteland'. It is not difficult to recognise the deep irony in the choice of such a site, and its former use, offering a commentary on the football I, as a supporter, had been exposed to over the years.

As with the fall of the Berlin Wall and the breakup of the Soviet Union, change for my football club happened quickly. The development came against a background of a wider questioning of stadia safety following the disasters of Hillsborough, Bradford, and Heysel during the 1980s. The tragedy of lost human lives could no longer be ignored. Fellows Park, the home of Walsall Football Club, was fast becoming a relic of the past, which was expensive to maintain and, worse, represented a potentially dangerous environment.

In 1989 the land upon which Fellows Park stood was sold, and the former Brockhurst Sewage Works, Bescot, a quarter of a mile away, was purchased. Extensive clearing of the site began in April 1989, followed by the construction of a new stadium to an industrial-looking blueprint previously used by Scunthorpe United. Football's first knight, Sir Stanley Matthews, officially opened the new stadium in August 1990. The team had by this time dropped into the lowest tier of League football but marked the occasion by playing a friendly against topflight neighbours Aston Villa. There were 9,500 in attendance, and the match was preceded by a carnival atmosphere that included a Caribbean-style steel band, cheerleaders, Scottish pipers, and a parachute team landing on the centre circle with the match ball.

Inevitably, Walsall lost the match heavily, not that this mattered, except to my oldest son, Jon. I had brought him to his first game. A Walsall game, and this was now his club. The pattern of initiation that I had experienced was replicated on a poor six-year-old boy[137]. Like my first game, the attendance was twice the normal average. The similarities however ended there. My first game had been in chilly weather, his was on a bright summer's afternoon. My first experience involved jostling for a good piece of concrete to stand on in a museum piece of a stadium that had grown organically over the best part of a century. My son had a ticket to a numbered seat set in a brand new, purpose-built, safe environment with near uninhibited views of a perfect playing surface.

Then there is the Yew Tree estate I once knew. In the fifties it represented an exciting project for newlyweds to build a society together. Now the notion of society has been challenged[138], and the demographic profile of residents, including age, ethnicity, and marital status, has broadened. The conceptual divides on the estate between the Walsall and West Bromwich clans no longer exist. Further, the privately owned and rented council housing divisions are irrelevant since the sale of council housing began

---

137 Against her better judgement, my wife Stephanie was also there. Jon's younger brother, Alex, escaped the experience of a Walsall home game until a later date.

138 Margaret Thatcher, Conservative Prime Minister 1979–90, challenged by the notion of society in the modern age.

in the eighties. The estate is now over sixty years old, and inevitably it has a tired feel to it, but the houses that I remember as being uniformly boring have now developed an individuality. Loft conversions are visible, front gardens have made way for off-road car parking, extensions and porches have been built, and draughty windows and doors have been replaced by assorted designs of energy-efficient uPVC replacements. There is no trace of the monstrous Churchill Towers that used to dominate the landscape. The Council's high-rise experiment to provide a palace in the sky produced a lived experience that felt more like a prison in the sky. Demolition in 1996 was a welcome development, particularly in the light of the tragedy of Grenfell Towers twenty-one years later.

In July 2021, Yew Tree Primary School made the national news headlines by gaining what the press described as a 'landmark ruling' in the High Court. My alma mater had defeated the Education Secretary's attempt to force it to become an academy (an independent state-funded school). Television shots of the school came as something of a surprise to me, as the building was absolutely nothing like I remembered it. Little wonder, the building I remembered had been bulldozed and replaced by a more energy-efficient, suitable structure a few years earlier. I should not have been surprised. It is the way of the world that the buildings and facilities considered state-of-the art in one generation should become not fit for purpose and replaced a couple of generations down the line.

When I was growing up, the Black Country pointed to heroes from the past like 'Jumping' Joseph Darby, whose specialty was spring jumping huge lengths, and of course the champion fighter William Perry, the Tipton Slasher. Today there are living Black Country alumni such as music legend and former Led Zeppelin vocalist Robert Plant, comedian Frank Skinner, and Sir Lenny Henry (comedian and actor). Although they may not be 'A-listers' like Plant, Skinner or Henry, Yew Tree estate boasts ex-residents who have left a trace on popular culture. Ian Hill and K.K. Downing are two lads who grew up on the estate and went on to form the rock band Judas Priest. The group was synonymous with the birth of the music genre known as 'Heavy Metal'. A third former Yew Tree estate resident, Jimmy Driscoll, created the children's cartoon characters the 'Shoe People', which appeared on television in the late eighties and went on to gain a worldwide audience and sell twenty-five million books along the way. It is either significant or wholly coincidental that heavy metal is a nod to the Black Country's industrial heritage, and Shoe People offers a link to Walsall's past leather trade.

One final postscript relates to my ancestry. My paternal grandfather, Job, claimed that I was related to the Tipton Slasher, William Perry, who was his own grandfather. Quite recently I began looking through copies of family birth, marriage, and death certificates. Job was born in Bradley, a Black Country village, to George and Mary Perry in August 1889. George was at that time employed as an iron puddler, a demanding manual job that led to the conversion of pig iron into wrought iron. It also had the effect of foreshortening the life span of workers. George and Mary's wedding looked to have a whiff of 'shotgun' about it the previous December. Mary's family name at the time of their marriage was also Perry[139]. George's father was named William, as my grandfather Job claimed. The marriage certificate curiously records his 'rank or profession' as an ironworker. If this William Perry was the Tipton Slasher, the entry on the certificate would have been something like retired pugilist or publican. As the Tipton Slasher died in 1880 and was never an ironworker, claims of a direct lineage to the Black Country hero look dubious. With two people sharing the family name Perry, I

---

139 I know what you are thinking. I knew a Smith who married an unrelated Smith and Perry is a relatively common family name.

explored the possibility that Mary's father was William Perry, the Tipton Slasher. He was not.

An internet search revealed that the Slasher, William, was one of five children of Timothy Perry. William and his wife Ann Marie had a son called William Edward, who was born in 1854. So, there is a possibility that William Edward was the father of either George or Mary, my great, great grandparents and Job was a generation out. The dates do not quite 'fit' however. At the time of George and Mary's marriage, William Edward would have been only thirty-four years old, making it unlikely that he was the father of either of these ancestors of mine.

All of this is far too complicated. What I am sure of is that my great, great grandfather is indeed William Perry, but not **the** William Perry. There may be a connection, but the 'fact' that Job's grandfather was the Tipton Slasher was a lie. If this was a lie, how authentic are Job's other stories? Did his quick thinking thwart execution at his captured gun post? Did he really escape from a Prisoner of War camp? I will never know for sure, but I can guess. My conclusion is that Job Perry was a survivor of the bloody carnage of the Great War, a hard worker in a demanding industry, a colourful character, a hopeless parent, and a grandparent I never knew. Above everything else he was a great storyteller.

We each carry with us a box of memories; this is mine, sorted and sifted and put into some order. Nostalgia can function as a rose-tinted filter, distorting memories and encouraging sentimentality. I have tried to guard against this by including harder-edged stories involving racism, disasters, and the nuclear threat. I am an unremarkable person who happens to have lived through a remarkable time of change. My box contains a world that existed once but is fast vanishing, one that is increasingly unrecognisable from how things are today. When change is so unrelenting and extreme, it is easy to be blindsided to its magnitude unless you take time to reflect and record your experiences. That is what I have attempted here with events of the fifties and sixties providing a backdrop to life on a new suburban Black Country estate. I hope you enjoyed reading it.

# References


**An introduction**
- Gray, D. (2018) *Black boots and football pinks.* Bloomsbury.

**Chapter One**
- Anon (2021) *History of house prices in Britain.* Updated on 12 July 2022. Sunlife
- https://www.sunlife.co.uk/articles-guides/your-money/the-price-of-a-home-in-britain-then-and-now/ Accessed 16/09/2022.
- Anon (2022) *The story of Walsall: The Leather Industry.* Wolverhampton history and heritage site http://www.historywebsite.co.uk/articles/Walsall/industry1b.html Accessed 18/10/2022.
- Bentley, D. (2017) *Birmingham's great mysteries: Our favourite myths about the city.* BirminghamLive Birmingham Mail. https://www.birminghammail.co.uk/news/midlands-news/birmingham-myths-charlie-chaplin-tolkein-6741169 Accessed 18/10/2022.
- Chiltern Open Air Museum (2023) https://coam.org.uk/tag/1950s Accessed 29/04/2023.
- NHS (2020) *Asbestosis* https://www.nhs.uk/conditions/Asbestosis/ Accessed 16/09/2022.
- Williams, N. (1999) *A century of the Black Country.* Sutton Publishing Limited.

**Chapter Two**
- Anon (2022) *Flashpoints – Hungary, Berlin, Cuba.* BBC. BBC Bitesize https://www.bbc.co.uk/bitesize/guides/zyjv4wx/revision/3 Accessed 29/04/2023.
- Britannica (2023) *Suez Crisis Middle East (1956)* https://www.britannica.com/biography/Lester-B-Pearson Accessed 29/04/2023.

• History.com editors (2019) *United States withdraws offer of aid for Aswan Dam.* History https://www.history.com/this-day-in-history/united-states-withdraws-offer-of-aid-for-aswan-dam Accessed 18/10/2022.
• Tvedt, T. (2004) The Nile: *An Annotated Bibliography.* London/New York

**Chapter Three**

• Anon (2018) *1954: Housewives celebrate end of rationing, On this day.* BBC. http://news.bbc.co.uk/onthisday/hi/dates/stories/july/4/newsid_3818000/3818563.stm Accessed 14/10/2022.
• Anon (2023) *The story of Walsall. The Second World War.* History.co.uk
• http://historywebsite.co.uk/articles/Walsall/WW2.htm Accessed 01/05/2023.
• BBC (2005) *The People's War. The Blitz in Walsall.* BBC https://www.bbc.co.uk/history/ww2peopleswar/stories/78/a3880578.shtml Accessed 01/05/2023.
• Campbell, D. (2018) *The NHS at 70: how the Guardian marked the work of a complex, vital institution* 12/06/2018 Guardian https://www.theguardian.com/society/2018/jul/12/nhs-70-anniversary-health-coverage-project Accessed 02/10/2022.
• *Fishman, N. (2022) Union History. TUC.* http://unionhistory.info/timeline/1945_1960_2.php Accessed 26/09/2022.
• Humphrys, J. (2014) *A brief History of home ownership in Britain.* History Extra. https://www.historyextra.com/period/modern/a-brief-history-of-home-ownership-in-britain/ Accessed 26/09/2022.

**Chapter Four**

- Akpan, I. (2015) *The 1956 Women's March in Pretoria.* South African History online. Last Updated 12 August 2022. https://www.sahistory.org.za/article/1956-womens-march-pretoria Accessed 05/10/2022.
- Anon (2022) *Sellafield Ltd.* Gov.UK https://www.gov.uk/government/organisations/sellafield-ltd/about Accessed 05/10/2022.
- Blakemore, B. (2020) *How Nelson Mandela fought apartheid – and why his work is not complete.* National Geographic https://www.nationalgeographic.com/history/article/nelson-mandela-fought-apartheid-work-not-complete Accessed 05/10/2022.
- Britannica editors (2022) *Apartheid social policy.* Last Updated: 24/08/2022 https://www.britannica.com/topic/apartheid Accessed 05/10/2022.
- Britannica editors (2022) *Marilyn Monroe* Encyclopaedia Britannica https://www.britannica.com/biography/Marilyn-Monroe Accessed 30/09/2022.
- Butler, B. (1988) *The Football League. The first 100 years.* Colour Library Books.
- Marsh, D. (2022) *Elvis Presley* Encyclopaedia Britannica Updated 12/08/2022.
- https://www.britannica.com/biography/Elvis-Presley Accessed 30/09/2022.
- Springsteen, B. (2018) *Springsteen on Broadway.* Netflix.

**Chapter Five**

- Anon (2022) *Nuclear war: does it take luck or reasoning to avoid it? Lessons from the Cuban missile crisis, 60 years on.* The Conversation https://theconversation.com/nuclear-war-does-it-take-luck-or-reasoning-to-avoid-it-lessons-from-the-cuban-missile-crisis-60-years-on-191239 Accessed 14/10/2022.
- Augustin, E. (2020) *Cuba faces squeeze on food production as US oil sanctions bite a.* The Guardian.18/03/2020.

https://www.theguardian.com/world/2020/mar/18/cuba-food-production-us-oil-sanctions Accessed 07/09/2022.
- Campaign for Nuclear Disarmament (2022) https://cnduk.org/who/ Accessed 02/10/2022.
- History.com Editors (2019) *The Bay of Pigs invasion begins.* History.com A&E Television Networks https://www.history.com/this-day-in-history/the-bay-of-pigs-invasion-begins Accessed 14/10/2022.
- *Knightley, P. (2011) The Cambridge Spies.* BBC History.
- https://www.bbc.co.uk/history/worldwars/coldwar/cambridge_spies_01.shtml Accessed 07/09/2022.
- Llewellyn, J. and Thompson, S. (2020) *Cuba under Castro.* Alpha History. https://alphahistory.com/coldwar/cuba-under-castro/ Accessed 05/10/2022.
- Masood, E. (2019) *How we endured the McCarthy purges in US.* BBC News.13/05/2019 https://www.bbc.co.uk/news/world-us-canada-48218827 Accessed 07/09/2022.

**Chapter Six**
- Francis, M. (2013) *Harold Wilson's 'white heat of technology' speech 50 years on.* The Guardian https://www.theguardian.com/science/political-science/2013/sep/19/harold-wilson-white-heat-technology-speech Accessed 8/10/2022.
- Hauser, T. (2022) *Muhammed Ali American boxer.* Encyclopaedia Britannica https://www.britannica.com/biography/Muhammad-Ali-boxer Accessed 8/10/2022.
- History.com Editors (2022) *Bernard Baruch popularizes the term 'Cold War'.* History. https://www.history.com/this-day-in-history/bernard-baruch-coins-the-term-cold-war
- Jodrell Bank Observatory website https://www.jodrellbank.net Accessed 01/05/2023.
- Spector, R.H. (2022) *The Vietnam War* Encyclopaedia Britannica https://www.britannica.com/event/Vietnam-War Accessed 22/09/2022.

**Chapter Seven**
- Harrison, R. (2008) *Must know stories.* Scripture Union.

**Chapter Eight**
- Anon (2023) *25 Blackpool Illuminations facts.* Visit Blackpool https://www.visitblackpool.com/things-to-do/blackpool-illuminations-and-lightpool/25-blackpool-illuminations-facts/ Accessed 01/05/2023.
- Flintham, J. (2021) *The story behind Billy Butlin – the man who revolutionised British holidays.* Lincolnshire live 16/07/2021. https://www.lincolnshirelive.co.uk/news/local-news/story-behind-billy-butlin-man-5651436 Accessed 01/05/2023.
- Smith, S. (2021) *Appeal for old photographs of Walsall Illuminations to celebrate 70th anniversary.* 25/05/21. Express and Star https://www.expressandstar.com/news/local-hubs/walsall/2021/05/25/appeal-for-old-photographs-of-walsall-illuminations-to-celebrate-70th-anniversary/ Accessed 01/05/2023.

**Chapter Nine**
- Anon (2023) *Snuff – a brief history* Wilsons and Co. https://sharrowmills.com/pages/snuff-a-brief-history Accessed 01/05/2023.
- Smith, C. (2015) *Slasher: The true story of William Perry.* Arcos Design.

**Chapter Ten**
- Anon (2022) *A Short History of German and Italian POWs in Britain.* Imperial War Museum www.iwm.org.uk/history/a-short-history-of-german-and-italian-pows-in-britain Accessed 15/09/2022.
- Anon (2023) *What was the Berlin Wall and how did it fall?* IWM. Imperial War Museum https://www.iwm.org.uk/history/what-was-the-berlin-wall-and-how-did-it-fall Accessed 01/05/2023.

- Britannica editors (2022) *Desert Rats.* Encyclopaedia Britannica. https://www.britannica.com/topic/Desert-Rats-World-War-II Accessed 13/10/2022.
- Nawrat, C. and Hutchings, S. (1997) *The Sunday Times Illustrated History of Football.* Reed International.

**Chapter Eleven**

- Britannica (2022) *Decade French chronology* www.britannica.com/topic/decade-French-chronology Accessed 07/09/2022.
- Geoghegan, T. (2009) *How Sunday trading changed the UK.* BBC News Magazine. 27/09/09http://news.bbc.co.uk/1/hi/magazine/8224062.stm Accessed 01/05/2023.
- Goodhart, B. (2022) *'At 6pm every evening the screen went blank': the outlandish tale of the UK's TV blackout* The Guardian 16/02/2022 https://www.theguardian.com/tv-and-radio/2022/feb/16/at-6pm-every-evening-the-screen-went-blank-the-outlandish-tale-of-the-uks-tv-blackout Accessed 07/09/2022
- Wilson, A. N. (2009) *Religion of hatred: Why we should no longer be cowed by the chattering classes ruling Britain who sneer at Christianity.* Daily Mail www.alisonmorgan.co.uk/Articles/A %20N %20Wilson %20Religion %20of %20 hatred.pdf 11/04/09

**Chapter Twelve**

- Christiano, M. (2017) *How the Space Race gave us GPS technology.* All about circuits. https://www.allaboutcircuits.com/news/the-history-of-gps-space-era// Accessed 18/10/2022.
- Daniel, H. (2011) *Benefits Of Space Program.* Benefits of everything that matters. http://benefitof.net/benefits-of-space-program/ Accessed 14/10/2022.
- Francis, M. (2013) *Harold Wilson's 'white heat of technology' speech 50 years on.* The Guardian https://www.theguardian.com/science/political-science/2013/sep/19/

harold-wilson-white-heat-technology-speech
Accessed 8/10/2022.

- Kendall, G. (2019) *Your Mobile Phone vs. Apollo 11's Guidance Computer.* Real Clear Science 02/07/2019.
- https://www.realclearscience.com/articles/2019/07/02/your_mobile_phone_vs_apollo_11s_guidance_computer_111026.html Accessed 07/09/2022.
- Moffit, D. (2021) *The man who died trying to break the water speed record in the Lake District.* Lancs Live. 07/03/2021 https://www.lancs.live/news/local-news/man-who-died-trying-break-19954187. Accessed 02/01/2023.

**Chapter Thirteen**

- Anon (2023) *The Slave Trade and Abolition.* Historic England https://historicengland.org.uk/research/inclusive-heritage/the-slave-trade-and-abolition/ Accessed 05/05/2023.
- Gabel, M. (2023) *Creation of the European Economic Community.* Britannica.
- https://www.britannica.com/topic/European-Community-European-economic-association Accessed 05/05/2023.
- Hattersley, R. (2004) *John Wesley: A Brand From The Burning: The Life of John Wesley.* Little, Brown Book Group.
- McGuinness (2022) *All You Need Is The Summer Of Love: How 1967 Sparked A Revolution.* 21/06/2022
- https://www.udiscovermusic.com/in-depth-features/summer-of-love-1967/ Accessed 05/05/2023.
- Porter, L. (2020) *Out of austerity: The Festival of Britain 1951 – A History and Examination.* 02/07/2020 https://londontopia.net/columns/lauras-london/out-of-austerity-the-festival-of-britain-1951-a-history-and-examination/#:~:text=The%201951%20Festival%20of%20Britain%20was%20a%20post-war,the%20nation'%20to%20promote%20the%20feeling%20of%20recovery. Accessed 05/05/2023.

**Chapter Fourteen**
- BBC (2023) *On this day 20 July* http://news.bbc.co.uk/onthisday/hi/dates/stories/july/20/newsid_3728000/3728225.stm Accessed 15/05/2023.
- Britannica (2023) *Imperial Chemical Industries plc* https://www.britannica.com/topic/Imperial-Chemical-Industries-PLC Accessed 15/05/2023.
- Conger, C. (2023) *How Tupperware works?.* HowStuffWorks https://people.howstuffworks.com/tupperware2.htm Accessed 17/05/2023.
- Farrell, T. (2015) A history of McDonald's UK Letslookagain.com 17/05/2015 http://letslookagain.com/2015/05/a-history-of-mcdonalds-in-the-uk/ Accessed 17/05/2023.
- Minkes, A. L. and Tucker D. G. (1979) *J. A. Crabtree: A Pioneer of Business Management,* Business History, 21:2, 198-212 https://doi.org/10.1080/00076797900000027 Accessed 17/05/2023.
- Mittal, A. (2023) *What Is Bakelite?: The Plastic That Changed The World* PlasticRanger 13/04/2023 https://plasticranger.com/what-is-bakelite/ Accessed 17/05/2023.
- Morton, D. (2021) *Before McDonald' and Burger King, there was Wimpy - check out the 1970s menu and prices* Chronicle Live 01/12/2021. https://www.chroniclelive.co.uk/news/history/before-mcdonalds-burger-king-wimpy-22319944 Accessed 17/05/2023.

**Chapter Fifteen**
- Grandy, C. (2019) *How the Black and White Minstrel Show spent 20 years on the BBC?.* The British Academy https://www.thebritishacademy.ac.uk/blog/how-black-and-white-minstrel-show-20-years-bbc Accessed 14/10/2022.
- Hendy, D. (2022) *The Black and White Minstrel Show.* BBC 100. https://www.bbc.com/historyofthebbc/100-voices/people-nation-empire/make-yourself-at-home/the-black-and-white-minstrel-show Accessed 14/10/2022.

- Jeffries, S. (2014) *Britain's most racist election: the story of Smethwick, 50 years on.* The Guardian. https://www.theguardian.com/world/2014/oct/15/ britains-most-racist-election-smethwick-50-years-on Accessed 14/10/2022.

**Chapter Sixteen**
- Anon (2017) *The history &evolution of card payments – infographic.* Paymentsense.com. 21/01/2017 https://www.paymentsense.com/uk/blog/infographic-evolution-of-card-payments/ Accessed 29/05/2023.
- Anon (2018) *The history of the NHS in charts.* BBC News. 24/06/2018. https://www.bbc.co.uk/news/ health-44560590 Accessed 29/05/2023.
- Gosling, P. (1995) *Co-op to revive the 'divi' money-back scheme.* The Independent www.independent.co.uk/ news/business/coop-to-revive-the-divi-moneyback-scheme-1589379.html

**Chapter Seventeen**
- History.Com Editors (2020) *Cultural Revolution.* A&E Television Networks. 03/04/2020
- https://www.history.com/topics/asian-history/cultural-revolution Accessed 29/05/2023.
- Parker, B. (2022) *Wolverhampton's Trolleybuses.* History website http://www.historywebsite.co.uk/articles/buses/ trolleybus.htm Accessed 16/09/2022.

**Chapter Eighteen**
- Anon (2021) *Where did the barber pole come from?* National Association of Barbers. 11/11/2021
- https://nationalbarbers.org/where-did-the-barber-pole-come-from/ Accessed 29/05/2023.

**Chapter Nineteen**

- Anon (2017) A brief history of the driving laws in Britain. 09/01/2017 https://www.mcginley.co.uk/news/a-brief-history-of-the-driving-laws-in-britain/bp215/ Accessed 30/05/2023.
- Anon (2023) *John Donne.* Poetry Foundation https://www.poetryfoundation.org/poets/john-donne Accessed 30/05/2023.
- Axon, G. (2020) *1955 vs. 2020 – How UK roads have changed in 65 years – Axon's Automotive Anorak.* Goodwood Road and Racing 24/04/2020
- https://www.goodwood.com/grr/road/news/2020/4/1955-vs.-2020--how-uk-roads-have-changed-in-65-years/ Accessed 30/05/2023.
- Houghton, L. (2017) British Car Brands Names – List and Logos of Top UK cars. Globalcarbrands.com. www.globalcarsbrands.com/british-car-brands/ Accessed 30/05/2023.
- Kendall, L. and R.T. (2000) *Great Christian prayers.* Hodder Christian Books.
- Leibling, D. (2008) *Car ownership in Great Britain* October 2008 Royal Automobile Club Foundation for Motoring https://www.racfoundation.org/assets/rac_foundation/content/downloadables/car%20ownership%20in%20great%20britain%20-%20leibling%20-%2020171008%20-%20report.pdf Accessed 30/05/2023.

**Chapter Twenty**

- Anon (2020) *Cathy Come Home: The TV drama that put homelessness on the map* BBC News 14/01/2020 https://www.bbc.co.uk/news/av/uk-51100189 Accessed 30/05/2023.
- Anon (2020) *20 books that defined the 1960s* Penguin 11/08/2020
- https://www.penguin.co.uk/articles/2020/08/books-that-defined-the-1960s Accessed 30/05/2023.

- Brooke, M. (2022) *The "Angry Young Men"* BFI Screen Online http://www.screenonline.org.uk/film/id/594201/index.html Accessed 02/10/2022.

**Chapter Twenty-one**
- Anthony, A. (2013) *A history of television, the technology that seduced the world – and me.* The Guardian 07/09/2013 https://www.theguardian.com/tv-and-radio/2013/sep/07/history-television-seduced-the-world Accessed 30/05/2023.
- Bates, S. (2022) *From rationing to reality TV – how Britain and the monarchy changed in Elizabeth's lifetime.* The Guardian. https://www.theguardian.com/uk-news/2022/sep/10/from-rationing-to-reality-tv-how-britain-and-the-monarchy-changed-in-elizabeths-lifetime Accessed 02/10/2022.
- Blakemore, E. (2020) *How the 1966 Aberfan Mine Disaster Became Elizabeth II's Biggest Regret* History.com 14/12/2020 https://www.history.com/news/elizabeth-ii-aberfan-mine-disaster-wales Accessed 30/05/2023.
- Channel 4 (2022) *1966: Who Stole the World Cup?* Channel 4. 04/11/2022.
- Inglis, S. (2006) *The best of Charles Buchan's Football Monthly.* English Heritage and Football Monthly Ltd.
- Nawrat, C. and Hutchings, S. (1997) *The Sunday Times Illustrated History of Football.* Hamlyn.
- Stevens, R. (2016) *How Pickles the dog found the World Cup trophy - 50 years on.* BBC Sport. https://www.bbc.co.uk/sport/football/35872662 Accessed 02/10/2022.

**Chapter Twenty-two**
- Walsall FC (1966) The *Saddlers News* Matchday programme Walsall v St. Neots Town

**The big tidy up**

- Anon (2021) *Walsall primary school wins 'landmark ruling' over academy order.* BBC. 23/07/2021. https://www.bbc.co.uk/news/uk-england-birmingham-57944481 Accessed 30/05/2023.
- Augustin, E. (2020) *Cuba faces squeeze on food production as US sanctions bite* The Guardian 18/03/2020. https://www.theguardian.com/world/2020/mar/18/cuba-food-production-us-oil-sanctions Accessed 30/05/2023.
- Hall, R. (2019) *Red Menace.* BBC 4.
- Kirk-Wade, E. (2023) *UK Defence Expenditure* 20/04/2023. House of Commons Library https://commonslibrary.parliament.uk/research-briefings/cbp-8175/ Accessed 30/05/2023.
- Nawrat, C. and Hutchings, S. (1997) *The Sunday Times Illustrated History of Football.* Hamlyn
- Pedley, D. (2013) *Defender of the Faith: K.K. Downing talks exclusively to The Midlands Rocks.* The Midlands Rocks http://www.themidlandsrocks.com/defender-of-the-faith-k-k-downing-talks-exclusively-to-the-midlands-rocks/ Accessed 14/10/2022.
- Poole, A., Walsall FC (2010) *The Bescot Years 1990-2010.* Excel Print Ltd.

# The author

Bob, happily married to wife Stephanie, is blessed that his two sons and two grandsons live close by. Retired after 25 years as a local university academic, he resides just outside the Black Country, enjoying countryside views.

Bob has written academic papers and professional body learning materials in the past, but this is his first "real" book. In his late sixties, Bob was struck by the fact that he had lived through a significant and sometimes dangerous period of history. Building on clear memories of his early years, Bob interweaves the mundane from a world that is fast disappearing and sets it within the context of significant events of the time. Bob is an unremarkable person who happens to have lived through a remarkable time of change. He has crafted his story, but it also echoes the story of every baby boomer. For those much younger, it is an opportunity to lift the lid on a time capsule, to open a door into another world.